Mines and Minerals of Siskiyou County California

by California Bureau of Mines

with an introduction by Kerby Jackson

Introduction

It has been years since the California Bureau of Mines released his important publication "Mines and Minerals of Siskiyou County California". First released in 1931, this important volume has now been out of print for this days and has been unavailable to the mining community since those days, with the exception of expensive original collector's copies and poorly produced digital editions.

It has often been said that "*gold is where you find it*", but even beginning prospectors understand that their chances for finding something of value in the earth or in the streams of the Golden West are dramatically increased by going back to those places where gold and other minerals were once mined by our forerunners. Despite this, much of the contemporary information on local mining history that is currently available is mostly a result of mere local folklore and persistent rumors of major strikes, the details and facts of which, have long been distorted. Long gone are the old timers and with them, the days of first hand knowledge of the mines of the area and how they operated. Also long gone are most of their notes, their assay reports, their mine maps and personal scrapbooks, along with most of the surveys and reports that were performed for them by private and government geologists. Even published books such as this one are often retired to the local landfill or backyard burn pile by the descendents of those old timers and disappear at an alarming rate. Despite the fact that we live in the so-called "Information Age" where information is supposedly only the push of a button on a keyboard away, true insight into mining properties remains illusive and hard to come by, even to those of us who seek out this sort of information as if our lives depend upon it. Without this type of information readily available to the average independent miner, there is little hope that our metal mining industry will ever recover.

This important volume and others like it, are being presented in their entirety again, in the hope that the average prospector will no longer stumble through the overgrown hills and the tailing strewn creeks without being well informed enough to have a chance to succeed at his ventures.

Kerby Jackson
Josephine County, Oregon
March 2017

MINES AND MINERAL RESOURCES OF SISKIYOU COUNTY

By J. C. O'Brien*

OUTLINE OF REPORT

ILLUSTRATIONS

INTRODUCTION

Geography

Siskiyou County is one of the three northermost counties of California. It borders on the state of Oregon for some 110 miles and is bounded on the west by Del Norte and Humboldt Counties, on the east by Modoc County, and on the south by Shasta and Trinity Counties. It is from 60 to 70 miles wide and has an area of 4,040,320 acres, of which about 68 percent is in the public domain. The Klamath National Forest

* District Mining Engineer, California State Division of Mines. Manuscript submitted for publication June 30, 1947.

alone has an area of 1,291,619 acres; Shasta National Forest, 712,168 acres; and Modoc National Forest 92,419 acres, within the county.

Siskiyou County had a population of 28,598 according to the 1940 census. Yreka, the county seat, is located on U. S. Highway 99 about the center of the county. A branch line about 7 miles long connects it with the mainline of the Southern Pacific Railway at Montague.

Topography

The region is mountainous throughout the western half of its area but several valleys in the central and east-central sections include about one-fifth of the total area, and farming ranks second to lumbering as a basic industry. The Klamath Mountains cover approximately the western half of the county and include the Siskiyou, Salmon, Marble, and Scott Bar ranges. These are among the wildest and most rugged in California. Prominent peaks and ridges rise 6000 to 8000 feet above sea level. The drainage is transverse and irregular, having developed on an uplifted plateau. The Klamath River flows west and south through deep, rocky canyons, and has left many gold-bearing gravel benches, terraces, and bars along its course. Its principal tributaries, the Shasta, Scott, and Salmon Rivers, flow in a generally northwesterly direction and each in turn has numerous forks and tributaries which have been mined for their gold-bearing gravels.

The Cascade Range is wholly of volcanic origin and includes a chain of cones in the central and east-central portion of the county. Mount Shasta, the most prominent cone, elevation 14,162 feet, is the second highest mountain in the state. Glass Mountain on the western border of the Cascade Range is a huge mass of black obsidian and glass flows, and has many square miles of pumice and volcanic cinder beds along its edges.

The eastern boundary of the county includes a portion of the Modoc Plateau, elevation 4000 to 6000 feet above sea level. It is an area covered by thick lava and tuff beds that have issued from numerous small volcanic cones and vents and is the southern extension of the volcanic plateau that covers eastern Oregon and southeastern Washington.

The low valley areas have warm summers and mild winters with little snowfall. The mountain areas are cool, and some of the high peaks are snow covered until late summer. The annual precipitation averages 50 inches or more in the extreme western areas and decreases to about 10 inches in the northeastern corner of the county.

Transportation

The main line of the Southern Pacific Railway crosses the central part of Siskiyou County from north to south, and there are a few short feeder lines to the east. U. S. Highway 99 follows along the railroad for most of its length across the county. U. S. Highway 97 leaves Highway 99 at Weed and runs northeastward through the county to Klamath Falls. State Highway 96 leaves U. S. Highway 99 where it crosses the Klamath River about 9 miles north of Yreka, follows the river westward and southward to Somes Bar and joins U. S. Highway 299 at Willow Creek in Humboldt County. The U. S. Forest Service has built roads along the principal rivers and forks, making it possible to drive an automobile or truck to many areas reached only by trail a few years ago. Many primitive areas are still left in the county, where scarcely a trail exists.

The eastern half of Siskiyou County is included in the Cascade Range and Modoc Plateau geomorphic provinces. The Geologic Map of California (Jenkins, O. P. 38) shows it to be covered with Tertiary and Quaternary volcanics, Pleistocene lake beds and Recent alluvium. Building stone, crushed rock, and pumice are mined in this area.

The western half of the county is within the Klamath Mountains province and the geologic formations and mineral deposits are similar to those found in the Sierra Nevada province. Its geologic history is described by J. S. Diller (14, pp. 13-14) as follows:

"Little is known of the early geologic history of the Klamath Mountain region, yet it is evident that in pre-Devonian [Diller, J. S. 03, p. 343], possibly in Algonkian [Hershey, O. H. 01, p. 245] or late Archean [Hershey, O. H. 12, p. 273] time the region was beneath the ocean, receiving the sediments from which the mica schist and intercalated crystalline limestones of South Fork Mountain and the Salmon Mountains north of Weaverville were formed.

"The extensive development of Devonian and Carboniferous shales, sandstones, cherts, and limestones in the Klamath Mountain region shows that at least a part of the region continued beneath the sea through the whole or the greater part of the Paleozoic era, but the incompleteness of the succession and the discordance among the formations bear evidence of considerable earth movements at several times during the long period of sedimentation, culminating in the great mountain-building epoch at the close of the Jurassic. At times, too, while these sedimentary rocks were forming, especially before the Middle Devonian and during the later part of the Carboniferous and the greater portion of the Mesozoic, volcanoes were active in the region, giving rise to extensive sheets of contemporaneous lava and tuff intermingled with the sedimentary rocks and in many places covering them.

"About the close of the Jurassic period this complex of sedimentary and igneous rocks was compressed, folded, faulted and uplifted to form the Klamath Mountains, and at the culmination of this process the mass was intruded by coarse granular bodies of plutonic rocks, such as granodiorite, gabbro, and peridotite, and by many dikes having a wide range in chemical and mineral composition.

"As a consequence of this intense, varied, and long-continued igneous action, the heated circulating waters finally formed many ore deposits within the intruded masses or near their contacts. These deposits may have been enriched later by descending waters from the zone of oxidation.

"Erosion and subsidence during the Cretaceous period reduced the Klamath Mountains to sea level, and for a brief interval they may have been completely covered by the ocean, for remnants of a once continuous sheet of conglomerates, sandstone, and shale are widely distributed in the region.

"At the close of Cretaceous time the Klamath Mountains were again uplifted, and with a number of later oscillations and the consequent erosion they have been carved to their present form by streams, which have concentrated the gold in the auriferous gravels."

MINES AND MINERAL RESOURCES

Production Statistics

The mines of Siskiyou County between 1880 and 1945 yielded mineral products valued at $50,830,383. Several million dollars worth of gold were probably mined before 1880, when mineral statistics were first recorded. Although gold has been by far the principal mineral produced, some 16 other mineral products including asbestos, chromite, coal, copper, gem stones, lead, limestone, manganese, marble, mineral water, platinum, pumice, quicksilver, sandstone, silver, and miscellaneous stone, have contributed to the total. The mines and mineral deposits that have shown some activity since the last Siskiyou County report of the Division of Mines (Averill, C. V. 35) are described in the following pages. A few that have been idle are included because of their past prominence.

Year	Gold, value	Silver, value	Chromite		Mineral water	
			Tons	Value	Gallons	Value
1880	$440,735	$95,340				
1881	850,000	1,500				
1882	720,000					
1883	400,000					
1884	475,000					
1885	338,659					
1886	342,677	64				
1887	606,859	177				
1888	625,000					
1889	915,294	370				
1890	860,303	23				
1891	957,220	120				
1892	1,013,332	56				
1893	799,108					
1894	760,782					
1895	950,006	177			200,000	$80,800
1896	1,091,265	653			[3]	
1897	842,123	34			[3]	
1898	768,804	321			[3]	
1899	991,771	100			[3]	
1900	951,397	[2]6,700			700,000	45,000
1901	886,043	[2]2,980			700,000	175,000
1902	906,989	233			750,000	187,500
1903	613,576	22			750,000	50,000
1904	892,685	1,230			750,000	50,000
1905	803,035	2,499			[3]	
1906	[3]	[3]			[3]	
1907	398,017	3,037			725,000	36,250
1908	504,156	6,125			700,000	80,000
1909	416,160	2,145			500,000	10,000
1910	437,376	2,322			500,000	60,000
1 11	422,297	2,561			700,000	120,000
1912	472,314	2,980	220	$2,310	700,000	120,000
1913	[4]180,125	[4]1,228			700,000	120,000
1914	312,842	1,026			650,000	65,000
1915	426,716	2,081	[3]		626,680	62,990
1916	441,307	2,312	2,251	28,731	502,650	50,530
1917	325,550	16,883	2,046	49,797	503,000	50,600
1 18	294,227	14,501	6,612	336,588	501,750	50,175
1919	226,525	17,049	510	13,379	451,500	90,375
1920	80,707	5,218	215	5,732	300,150	60,015
1921	42,635	294	[3]		250,150	5,015
1922	75,105	612				
1923	45,633	298			200,150	4,042
1924	63,570	296				6,100
1925	180,120	831			[3]	
1926	141,240	709			[3]	

| Platinum-group metals | | Miscellaneous stone[1], value | Miscellaneous and unapportioned | | |
Ounces	Value		Amount	Value	Substance
--------	--------	--------	--------	--------	
--------	--------	--------	--------	--------	
--------	--------	--------	--------	--------	
--------	--------	--------	--------	--------	
--------	--------	--------	--------	--------	
--------	--------	--------	--------	--------	
--------	--------	--------	--------	--------	
--------	--------	--------	--------	--------	
--------	--------	--------	--------	--------	
100	$600	--------	--------	--------	
--------	--------	--------	--------	--------	
--------	--------	--------	--------	--------	
--------	--------	--------	--------	--------	
--------	--------	--------	--------	$1,202,742	Unapportioned, 1900-09.
--------	--------	--------	200 lbs.	23	Copper.
--------	--------	--------	--------	--------	
1.6	21	--------	--------	--------	
5.3	93	--------	2,500 cu. ft.	1,250	Sandstone.
			2,500 cu. ft.	1,500	Sandstone.
			193 lbs.	39	Copper.
			2,643 lbs.	140	Lead.
--------	--------	$39,000	11,433 cu. ft.	12,897	Sandstone.
			1,000 bbls.	1,000	Lime.
			2 20 tons	300	Limestone.
			4,949 lbs.	1,183	Lead.
			1,800 cu. ft.	1,485	Sandstone.
			1,090 lbs.	1,680	Lime.
			3,360 lbs.	144	Lead.
			50 tons	500	Pumice.
--------	--------	5,028	1,050 cu. ft.	1,750	Sandstone.
			100 bbls.	300	Lime.
			2,225 tons	2,200	Limestone.
				14,745	Gems.
--------	--------	9,475	1,204 cu. ft.	2,000	Sandstone.
			335 bbls.	735	Lime.
			35 tons	525	Limestone.
				1,000	Gems.
--------	--------	6,580	150 bbls.	120	Lime.
			24 tons	24	Limestone.
			650 cu. ft.	455	Sandstone.
--------	--------	609	250 cu. ft.	250	Sandstone.
				250	Gems.
				250	Gems.
--------	--------	4,883	90 tons	2,000	Pumice.
				1,500	Other minerals.
			100 tons	500	Coal.
9	304	5,371	58 lbs.	2	Lead.
			677 bbls.	629	Lime.
			250 cu. ft.	150	Sandstone.
--------	--------	4,630	188 lbs.	9	Lead.
			745 bbls.	745	Lime.
2	--------	45,407		16,923	Chromite, copper, marble, sandstone.
			--------	12,609	Copper, building stone, lime, platinum, sandstone.
				500	Granite.
15	709	134,382	888,043 lbs.	242,436	Copper.
			192 lbs.	17	Lead.
				8,535	Lime, sandstone, soda.
1	58	24,588	573,593 lbs.	141,677	Copper.
				15,473	Lead and pumice.
7	1,015	26,405	--------	111,294	Copper, limestone, pumice, quicksilver.
		30,322		47,121	Copper, lime, limestone, potash, pumice, quicksilver.
2	--------	44,343		1,060	Asbestos, brick, chromite, lime, platinum.
		21,726		4,020	Other minerals.[5]
3	339	129,291		1,408	Other minerals.[6]
--------	--------	67,787		3,034	Other minerals.[7]
2	--------	23,800		3,535	Lime and limestone.
				11,340	Mineral water, platinum, sandstone.
16	1,780	327,569	--------	22,853	Coal, lead, mineral water, sandstone.

Year	Gold, value	Silver, value	Chromite		Mineral water	
			Tons	Value	Gallons	Value
1927	$138,822	$586			²	
1928	85,717	421			³	
1929	63,843	863			³	
1930	70,332	4,172			³	
1931	74,326	169			³	
1932	133,115	304			³	
1933	324,954	686			²	
1934	528,395	1,861			³	
1935	575,676	1,610			³	
1936	639,030	2,873				
1937	1,055,600	3,420			³	
1938	1,294,230	3,335			³	
1939	1,708,840	5,196	³		³	
1940	2,068,815	6,651			³	
1941	2,351,790	7,135	³		³	
1942	1,356,530	4,187	³		²	
1943	110,040	6,712	³		²	
1944	128,870	10,203	2,225	$89,650	³	
1945	93,345	1,799	³		³	
Totals	$38,091,555	$257,290	14,079	$526,187	³12,361,030	$1,579,392

Grand total value, $50,830,383.

[1] Includes crushed rock, rubble, rip-rap, sand, gravel.
[2] Recalculated to 'commercial,' from 'coining value' as originally published.
[3] See under 'Unapportioned.'
[4] Production from dredging operations included in Stanislaus County production.
[5] Includes limestone and mineral water.
[6] Includes lead and lime.
[7] Includes coal, limestone, lime and platinum.

Asbestos

The industries of World War II created a great demand for all types of asbestos, and during the war prospectors were urged to search for deposits in the serpentine areas of Siskiyou County. No new deposits were discovered, however, and there was no production from the previously known prospects and occurrences.

Chamberlain (Burns) Ranch includes 800 acres of patented land about 4 miles west of Gazelle in secs. 16, 17, 20, T. 42 N., R. 6 W., owned by C. C. Chamberlain. A light-green, brittle, chrysotile asbestos occurs in dark-green serpentine bands up to three-eighths of an inch wide. It has been exposed in a trench 5 feet wide, 20 feet long, and 3 feet deep. The mineral rights to this property are under lease to Ray J. Sylvester of Weed. (Logan 25, p. 421; Averill 35, p. 264.)

C. C. Cady prospect on Greenhorn Mountain, between Yreka and Fort Jones has not been developed since 1935. (Logan 25, p. 421; Averill 35, p. 264.)

Platinum-group metals		Miscellaneous stone[1], value	Miscellaneous and unapportioned		
Ounces	Value		Amount	Value	Substance
10	$690	$102,428	----------	$56,420	Mineral water, sandstone.
		370,833	----------	14,195	Copper, lead, gems (rhodonite), mineral water.
		110,878	----------	54,205	Copper, lead, limestone, quicksilver, mineral water.
		85,851	----------	75,046	Copper, lead, granite, mineral water, gems, platinum quicksilver, lime, pumice.
		79,772	----------	32,740	Other minerals.
		23,415	----------	27,185	Lead, quicksilver, mineral water.
		29,036	----------	19,502	Copper, lead, mineral water, pumice.
		67,216	----------	50,694	Copper, lead, mineral water, pumice, tube-mill pebbles.
3		66,664	----------	61,787	Copper, mineral water, pumice, tube-mill pebbles.
			1,805 lbs.	166	Copper.
		106,182	6,088 tons	49,200	Pumice.
			----------	33,652	Lead, mineral water, platinum, tube-mill pebbles.
		103,519	1,168 lbs.	144	Copper.
			----------	37,668	Lead, gems, mineral water, pumice, quicksilver, tube-mill pebbles.
3		116,331	----------	96,919	Copper, lead, mineral water, platinum, pumice, tube-mill pebbles.
3		99,906	701 tons	5,169	Pumice.
			----------	30,884	Chromite, mineral water, platinum, tube-mill pebbles.
3		102,923	637 tons	2,250	Pumice and scoria.
			----------	38,564	Copper, mineral water, platinum.
3		141,439	7,132 tons	16,330	Pumice.
			----------	61,531	Chromite, copper, lead, mineral water, platinum, quicksilver.
3		105,952	7,668 lbs.	928	Copper.
			----------	152,917	Chromite, gems, lead, mineral water, pumice, quicksilver, platinum.
		221,837	9,707,958 lbs.	1,262,035	Copper.
			----------	295,622	Chromite, manganese ore, mineral water, quicksilver.
		96,369	15,856,568 lbs.	2,140,637	Copper.
			----------	42,195	Manganese ore, mineral water, pumice.
			4,042,886 lbs.	545,787	Copper.
		145,327	5,230 tons	36,470	Pumice.
			----------	103,577	Chromite, diatomite, limestone, mineral water.
167.9	$5,609	$3,127,074	----------	$7,243,276	

Shasta View prospect in sec. 8, T. 41 N., R. 5 W., consists of 12 unpatented claims owned by William W. Gassoway and George C. Taylor. They are leased to Ray J. Sylvester of Weed. Mr. W. S. Russell of Edgewood is reported to have produced several tons of fiber from these claims in 1921. Bands of green, brittle, asbestos with fibers up to three-fourths of an inch long occur in zones in peridotite. On the Shasta View claim an adit striking N. 15° W. is caved near the portal. About 50 tons of material on the dump showed fiber one-sixteenth of an inch long in bands spaced from a quarter to three-quarters of an inch apart. The claims have been prospected by several shallow pits and trenches. (Logan 25, p. 421; Averill 35, p. 265.)

Chromite

Chromite mining was resumed in Siskiyou County in 1939 after a lapse of 18 years. Production came from small lenses of high-grade ore found in the peridotite, serpentine, and dunite rocks which outcrop over a large area in the western part of the county.

The Metals Reserve Company established a stockpile at Yreka in the spring of 1942 for the purchase of small lots of chrome and manganese ores. Specifications and price schedules were revised from time to time until May 15, 1943, when ores and concentrates containing a minimum of 35 percent chromic oxide and having a chromium to iron ratio not less than 1.5 to 1 were accepted in lots of 10 or more long tons. Purchases were continued at the Yreka stockpile until December 31, 1945. This made it possible for many small deposits to be mined by individuals employing from one to ten men. All of the ore was hand sorted and some of the banded and disseminated ores were hand cobbed before shipment. A great deal of the material discarded as too low grade for shipment might have been made into an acceptable concentrate by a gravity milling process.

Barkhouse and Whiskey Boy claims in sec. 11, T. 46 N., R. 11 W., M. D., are owned by A. Lowden of Seiad and leased to K. W. Walters of Happy Camp. About 30 tons of lump chromite were mined from lenses in serpentine on this property in 1943. (O'Brien 43a, p. 328.)

Black Crow and Black Hawk claims (Eldridge) are owned by Virgil Gray and Tom Eldridge of Cecilville, who produced a few tons of chromite from lenses in serpentine in sec. 20, T. 38 N., R. 11 W., M. D. (O'Brien 43a, p. 328.)

Browne Ranch is in sec. 1, T. 41 N., R. 9 W., M. D. Fred P. Browne, owner, shipped 16 tons of chromite from small lenses in serpentine in 1942.

Burton Ranch in sec. 24, T. 44 N., R. 8 W., M. D., is owned by Fred C. Burton of Yreka. Shipments of chromite were made from small lenses in serpentine on this property by J. R. Allison, Clem Baker, Fred W. Burton, William McCoy, Oliver W. Costello, and H. S. Schell and son. Twenty tons of ore, said to have assayed 54 percent Cr_2O_3 with a 2.9 to 1 chromium to iron ratio, were shipped to the Metals Reserve Company stockpile at Yreka in 1945. (O'Brien 43, p. 82.)

Coggins mine in sec. 35, T. 39 N., R. 4 W., M. D., is owned by Arthur L. Coggins of Ashland, Oregon. The U. S. Forest Service built 2 miles of road to this property. Sixteen shallow holes were diamond drilled by the U. S. Bureau of Mines in 1942-43, and an estimated 1000 tons of shipping-grade chromite developed. The property was operated in 1942-43 by James K. Remsen of Grants Pass, Oregon, under a sub-lease from the Rustless Mining Corporation. Massive chromite occurring in lenses in dunite was mined from an adit 212 feet long driven in a N. 17° W. direction. Broken, shifting ground required heavy timbering. Remsen shipped 1,926 tons of chromite worth $32 to $33 per ton to the Sacramento stockpile. Ten men were employed on two shifts under Manley Brown, manager.

In 1943, Hugh Williamson of Redding drove a new adit about 40 feet below the old caved workings on this property and shipped an additional 200 tons to the stockpile. (Averill 35, pp. 266, 269; Allen 41, p. 129; O'Brien 43, p. 82; 43a, p. 328; Bradley 18, pp. 191-193.)

Constable and Foster claims are located in sec. 1, T. 41 N., R. 7 W., M. D. Hugh Williamson of Redding mined chromite from a timbered open cut about 70 feet long in a N. 65° E. direction, 4 feet wide and about 18 feet deep, and from an adit driven S. 70° E. for about 30 feet. The chromite had an average width of 2 feet between serpentine walls. The ore was trucked 30 miles to the Yreka stockpile and is said to have averaged 50 percent Cr_2O_3 with a 3 to 1 chromium to iron ratio. (O'Brien 43a, p. 327.)

Costello mine in sec. 24, T. 44 N., R. 8 W., was owned and operated by Oliver W. Costello of Yreka, who shipped 20 tons of lump chromite in 1942.

Cyclone Gap (Mammoth) mine consists of two claims in S½ sec. 15, T. 17 N., R. 5 E., H. The U. S. Forest Service built 22 miles of access road from Waldo, Oregon, to this property in 1942. An irregular body of chromite measuring about 25 feet long, 20 feet thick, and about 60 feet deep occurred in dunite and serpentine. It was mined by open cuts and an adit striking S. 55° E., 110 feet from which raises, stopes, and a winze 26 feet deep were driven to extract the ore. The chromite was hand sorted and trucked 64 miles to the Grants Pass stockpile. James K. Remsen of Grants Pass, Oregon, mined about 2000 tons of 43 to 45 percent Cr_2O_3 from this deposit in 1942. Eight men were employed under Ben Baker, superintendent. (O'Brien 43, p. 82; 43a, p. 328.)

Doe Creek deposit is in W½ sec. 32, T. 17 N., R. 5 E., H. It is owned by Homer White and Jim Hoge of Kerby, Oregon. Two lenses of chromite in serpentine were mined by open cuts. One eastward-trending lens was about 42 feet long, 9 feet wide, and from 15 to 20 feet deep. Another lens, about 100 feet to the northwest, measured about 18 feet in length, 15 feet in width, and 8 feet in depth. In 1942 this property was leased to J. B. Isgrid of Grants Pass, and G. P. Lily of Baker, Oregon. In October 1942 nine men were employed under B. F. O'Frary, superintendent, and about 1500 tons of 38 percent Cr_2O_3 with a 3 to 1 chromium to iron ratio had been produced. The ore was trucked 105 miles to the stockpile at Grants Pass, Oregon.

In August 1944 Linkhart and Messinger of Kerby, Oregon, had a lease on this property. Two men were employed sinking on a lens from which they had mined about 150 tons. (Maxson 33, pp. 139, 153; Allen 41, p. 123; O'Brien 43, p. 82.)

Dry Gulch mine, five claims in sec. 16, T. 38 N., R. 11 W., M. D., is owned by Luther Lake and his wife, and V. A. Gray of Cecilville. About 150 tons of high-grade lump chromite was mined from six small lenses in serpentine at this property in 1944-45.

Fairview Chrome mine, four claims in secs. 27 and 34, T. 46 N., R. 11 W., M. D., was purchased in 1942 by F. S. Pollak of Washington, D. C., from Mrs. Dorothea Reddy Moroney of Yreka. Chromite occurred in parallel bands and disseminated through a tan-colored dunite in a zone about 100 feet wide near the top of a ridge about 3½ miles northwest of Hamburg. It was mined from open cuts and from stopes above an adit driven N. 25° W. following a band of chromite about 2 feet wide. The chromite was hand sorted and cobbed from the dunite before shipping to the Yreka stockpile. From six to fifteen men were employed under H. E. Ellickson, manager. Production continued from the summer of 1942 to the fall of 1945 except for interruptions caused by bad roads in the winter. The grade averaged from 35 to 40 percent Cr_2O_3 with a 2.4 to 1 chromium to iron ratio. Much low-grade disseminated material was discarded. (O'Brien 43, p. 82; U. S. Geological Survey 43, p. 94; O'Brien 43a, p. 328.)

Flederman lease, in sec. 9, T. 44 N., R. 7 W., M. D., is owned by the Southern Pacific Land Company. Max Erwin of Yreka shipped about 30 tons of 51 percent Cr_2O_3 from this property in 1942. The chromite occurred in small lenses in serpentine and was mined from an adit driven N. 40° W. about 75 feet.

Genesis (Hayden) claim, in sec. 35, T. 42 N., R. 7 W., M.D., is owned by Southern Pacific Land Company, and leased to R. V. Hayden of Callahan. Ernest Hayden and Charles Thompson of Callahan followed a lens of high-grade chromite in serpentine to a depth of 140 feet in a shaft inclined 70 degrees in a S. 67° W. direction. Ore from this shaft and from several other shallow shafts and pits averaged from 48 to 52 percent Cr_2O_3 with a 3.4 to 1 chromium to iron ratio. Shipments were made to the Yreka stockpile in 1942, 1943, and 1944. (O'Brien 43a, p. 328.)

Ladd (Red Mountain, Dolbear) mine, three claims in sec. 15, T. 46 N., R. 11 W., M.D., is owned by John Ladd of Seiad and leased to Mrs. Dorothea Reddy Moroney, Klamath River Post Office. The U. S. Forest Service built 4 miles of access road to this property in 1943. Chromite occurs disseminated and in bands in a tan-colored dunite. It was mined from short adits and shallow open cuts. Ronald Knudsen of Yreka had four men employed at this property in June 1943, building ore bins and a gravity tram 150 feet long, but only a small production of ore was made. There seemed to be a considerable quantity of low-grade chromite at this property. (O'Brien 43, p. 82; U. S. Geological Survey 43, p. 96; O'Brien 43a, p. 328.)

Lady Gray mine, three claims in sec. 30, T. 45 N., R. 10 W., M.D., is owned by Mrs. Dorothea Reddy Moroney of Klamath River Post Office. About 4 miles of access road was built to this property from the Scott Bar-Fort Jones highway. A 24-inch band of fine-grained chromite is said to assay 38 percent Cr_2O_3. From three to five men were employed in April 1945 building a road with a bulldozer and mining and stockpiling the ore from an open cut about 12 feet long, 11 feet wide, and 8 feet deep at the face. (O'Brien 43, p. 83.)

Lambert (Peg Leg) mine, in sec. 25, T. 44 N., R. 8 W., M.D., is owned by Basil Wild and Carl Johnson of Fort Jones. Flat lenses of high-grade chromite from 10 inches to 3 feet thick were mined from an adit driven S. 55° E. about 125 feet, and from bulldozer cuts along the bank. This property was mined under lease by C. F. Shaw of Yreka in January 1943. Three men were employed. In April 1945 the property was purchased by H. E. Ellickson and Nick Young of Yreka. A bench about 350 feet long, 70 feet wide, with a bank 10 to 15 feet deep, was cut with a bulldozer, during the mining and prospecting of this property. Chromite shipped to the Yreka stockpile is said to have assayed from 52 to 54 percent Cr_2O_3. (Logan 25, p. 424; Averill 35, p. 266; O'Brien 43, p. 83; 43a, p. 328.)

McGuffy Creek deposits, in sec. 25, T. 45 N., R. 11 W., M.D., and secs. 30 and 31, T. 45 N., R. 10 W., M.D., were mapped by the U. S. Geological Survey and drilled and sampled by the U. S. Bureau of Mines in 1942. Low-grade chromite occurs banded and disseminated in dunite over large areas. Some high-grade ore was mined from this area in 1918 but no production has been made since, because of the difficulty and expense of building a road to the area.

Seiad Valley deposit, four patented and 13 unpatented claims in secs. 7, 17, 18, 19 and 20, T. 47 N., R. 11 W., M.D., is owned by the Rustless Mining Corporation, a subsidiary of Rustless Iron and Steel Corporation, 3400 East Chase Street, Baltimore, Maryland. The U. S. Geological Survey and U. S. Bureau of Mines mapped and sampled this property in 1941. Diamond-drill holes 125 to 350 feet deep were drilled in a N. 30° E. direction, at about 80-foot intervals, for a length of 1380 feet. A drift from the west adit at an elevation of 3280 feet was continued for 200 feet. The U. S. Forest Service widened, graded, and improved

A, GRAY EAGLE COPPER COMPANY MILL
Near Happy Camp, Siskiyou County

B, CHENOWETH DREDGE
Klamath River near Hamburg, Siskiyou County

5—76940

A, HUNTINGTON MILL
At Middle Fork Mines, Siskiyou County

B, SINGLE-BUCKET DREDGE
Midland Company, Incorporated, Siskiyou County

A, SCANDIA NO. 1 DREDGE
On Horse Creek, Siskiyou County

B, YREKA GOLD DREDGING COMPANY DREDGE
Klamath River Near Seiad, Siskiyou County

A, CRUSHING AND SCREENING PLANT
Of Electro Lime and Chemical Company at Gazelle, Siskiyou County

B, PUMICE PIT
Of Glass Mountain Volcolite Company, Siskiyou County

C, PUMICE CRUSHING AND CARLOADING EQUIPMENT
Of Allen Miers at Tionesta

$7\frac{1}{2}$ miles of road from Seiad to the property, and continued the road up the mountain to the Cook and Green Pass.

Chromite occurs banded and disseminated in dunite over a large area. During World War I several thousand tons of hand-sorted chromite said to average 48 percent Cr_2O_3 was shipped from this property by Dr. Reddy of Medford, Oregon. In January 1943 the Kangaroo Mountain Chrome Company obtained a lease from the Rustless Mining Corporation. Selected zones where a marketable grade of ore could be mined were assigned to miners and the ore they produced was purchased on the dump for $6 a ton. All tools, equipment, air, and powder were furnished by the company. J. A. and W. H. Young, Elmer Weeks and his brother, and other groups mined chromite from open cuts and short adits under James H. Suddreth, manager for the company. The chromite was shipped 60 miles to the stockpile at Yreka. (Averill 35, pp. 267-269; O'Brien 43a, p. 329.)

Simas Ranch, sec. 35, T. 44 N., R. 8 W., M.D., is owned by A. T. Simas of Yreka. Clem and Ben Baker of Yreka mined small lots of chromite from lenses in serpentine on this property in January 1944.

Snowy Ridge claim, in sec. 21, T. 48 N., R. 9 W., M.D., was leased and operated by James K. Remsen of Grants Pass, Oregon in 1942-43. Chromite was shipped 55 miles by truck to the Grants Pass stockpile.

Wild and Johnson deposit. Basil Wild and Carl Johnson of Fort Jones leased the N$\frac{1}{2}$ sec. 19, T. 42 N., R. 8 W., M.D., from the Southern Pacific Land Company. They shipped 120 tons of 53 percent Cr_2O_3 to the Yreka stockpile in 1943. The chromite was mined with a bulldozer from lenses of serpentine. (O'Brien 43a, p. 329.)

Coal

Occurrences of lignite and sub-bituminous coal have been noted in the Tertiary formations which outcrop east of Hornbrook in T. 47 N., R. 5, 6 W., and in the northwest quarter of T. 46 N., R. 5 W., M.D.

Hagedorn Ranch Deposit. About 30 years ago an incline shaft was sunk 700 feet on a soft coal seam dipping flatly east on the Hagedorn Ranch, 5 miles south of Ager. Three drifts were driven north and south a maximum distance of 500 feet on the coal. The thickness of solid coal is said to average 2 feet in a coal measure 6 feet wide.

A production of 100 tons valued at $500 was reported from this deposit in 1914 when it was under lease to the Yreka Development Company. There has been no production or development since then. (Averill 35, p. 270; Logan 25, p. 426.)

Cooley Ranch. A hole drilled 130 feet deep on the Cooley Ranch is reported to have cut 11 feet of coal. A second hole was said to have cut 20 inches of coal at 95 feet. (Averill 35, p. 270; Logan 25, p. 426.)

Siskiyou Coal and Coke Company had leases on ranches in Shasta Valley in 1925. A diamond-drill hole on the Herr Ranch, about a quarter of a mile north from the second hole on the Cooley Ranch, cored through alternate layers of sandstone and shale for 110 feet. (Logan 25, p. 426; Averill 35, p. 270.)

Copper

The urgent need for copper during the war led to the re-examination of many deposits that have been known for years. Several prospects were developed to a small extent and others were sampled, but only the Gray

Eagle mine in the Happy Camp district actually produced. The value of the copper produced from this mine far exceeded the gold produced in Siskiyou County in 1943-44.

Big Blue Claims. Two claims in sec. 36, T. 40 N., R. 9 W., M.D., were relocated in 1942 by Suzanne H. Hartley. Six quartz veins outcrop on these claims, which were located in a northeasterly direction along the slope of the mountain. The veins are from 3 to 12 feet wide and strike S. 65° to 77° W. and dip 70° to 80° S. They are sheared and cracked parallel to their strike, probably because of the intrusions of diorite and periodotite with which they are in contact in some instances. Sulphide solutions deposited bornite, chalcocite, and some chalcopyrite in the seams and cracks. There has been some oxidation to form malachite and azurite. No pyrite was noted. Only shallow development has been done on these claims and no assays from representative samples were reported.

Blue Ledge mine includes 26 patented claims 33 miles southwest of Jacksonville, Oregon, in sec. 3, T. 47 N., R. 11 W., and sec. 34, T. 48 N., R. 11 W., M. D. It is owned by the Mexican Mining and Refining Company, 120 Broadway, New York, N. Y. During the last period of operation (1920), some 9000 tons of sorted ore, said to average 13.7 percent copper, 5.5 ounces of silver, and 0.1 of an ounce of gold, was shipped. A vein averaging 5 feet in width, striking north and dipping 60° W. was developed for a length of 1500 feet by drifts and four adits, and by raises and winzes. Chalcopyrite is the principal ore mineral and it occurs with pyrite. Both walls of the vein are micaceous schist.

The U. S. Geological Survey and U. S. Bureau of Mines mapped and sampled this property in 1942, but no report of their examination has been published to date. The owners estimated 240,000 tons of ore, averaging 4.8 percent copper, 0.35 of an ounce of gold, and 1.5 ounces of silver, were blocked out in 1920. (Brown 16, p. 817; Laizure 21, p. 530; Tucker 23, p. 8; Logan 25, p. 427; Averill 35, pp. 261, 271; Aubury 05, p. 108; Hamilton 22, pp. 12,14.)

Copper Creek (Blue Bell) group of six claims in sec. 31, T. 16 N., R. 8 E., H., is owned by I. D. Turner of Redding. On Copper Creek No. 1 claim, a vertical shaft about 12 feet deep cut through a shear zone in andesite 8 feet wide, in which there are three bands of copper minerals from 2 to 12 inches wide replacing pyrite. The bands strike N. 15° W. and dip 15 to 20° W. Chalcopyrite, malachite, and some sphalerite occur with pyrite. A sample across 8 feet is said to have assayed 3 percent copper and 1 percent zinc. The prospect is reached by a 1½-mile trail southeast from Elk Creek. It is idle except for assessment work.

Copper King group, in sec. 20, T. 40 N., R. 7 W., M.D., consists of four claims owned by Norma B. Wilson. They are developed by an adit driven N. 23° E. about 300 feet on a quartz vein 8 feet wide, which dips 73° W. Above the adit, an old shaft 15 feet deep is said to have yielded 50 tons of ore assaying 5 percent copper and $8 in gold. The principal copper mineral is chalcopyrite and it is associated with pyrite. Both walls are serpentine. In the summer of 1943 the property was leased by Max Erwin of Yreka. James K. Remsen of Grants Pass reopened and timbered some of the caved workings for examination and sampling, but no production resulted.

Copper Mountain Group. Five claims in the Dillon Creek district are owned by Forest Moore, A. W. Scott, and George Russell of Happy Camp. They are a relocation of the Virginia claims once owned by Hugh

Wright. These claims are said to have a very large gossan outcrop but their development has been handicapped because they have no access road.

Facey Mine. One patented claim in the SW¼ sec. 23, T. 41 N., R. 9 W., M.D., is owned by Facey Brothers of Etna. It was leased in 1941 to Elwood and W. B. Stewart of Etna. Three men were employed mining copper carbonate and oxides from a vein 3 feet wide striking S. 60° W., and dipping 77° N. Both walls were gray lime-shale. An old adit driven N. 70° W. for 80 feet had a narrow vein in the face and a raise 30 feet high. The property was equipped with a wooden ore bin 15 feet square and 11 feet deep. A single cylinder "hot head" engine converted as a compressor was driven by a four-cylinder Ford engine and supplied compressed air for a jackhammer. Tinken bits were used. The property was operated a very short time, and so far as is known, no ore shipments were made.

Gray Eagle (Dakin) mine, 32 claims, mostly patented, in secs. 13, 14, and 23, T. 17 N., R. 7 E., M.D., are owned by the Gray Eagle Copper Company, a subsidiary of the Newmont Mining Corporation, 14 Wall Street, New York, N. Y. When this mine closed in 1919, a million tons of copper ore were said to be blocked out. The current low price of copper and the high cost of operation, owing to the distance from railroad and smelter, made this reserve unprofitable to work.

The Gray Eagle Copper Company reopened the property in December 1941, with Robert J. Hendricks as manager, W. P. Goss as assistant manager, and a staff including Duncan L. King, mill superintendent; W. E. Meals, plant designer; H. J. Steele, mining engineer; Jack Widauf, mine foreman; E. H. Tucker, chief electrician; Howard Johnson, master mechanic; and F. A. Scheck, chief clerk and purchasing agent. The road up the mountain from Indian Creek was widened, graded, and improved for about 2 miles. Sites were graded for mine plant, camp, and office buildings. The No. 7 adit was widened to an 8- by 9-foot section; 35-pound rails were laid for 30-inch gauge track; a 6-inch air line and 2-inch water line were installed, as well as two armored cables carrying electric power at 440 volts.

The ore body was roughly almond shaped and about 800 feet long, 400 feet wide, and from 6 to 70 feet thick on the edges and in the center, respectively; dip was about 25° N. Chalcopyrite was the principal copper mineral and it was a replacement of pyrite in a pyritic schist.

A station was cut on the west side of the haulage-level adit, and a raise 240 feet high was run to the ore. The raise was timbered with 8- by 8-inch square timbers, and divided into a 6- by 5-foot hoisting compartment; a 3½- by 5-foot manway in which the 6-inch air line, 2-inch water lines, and 440-volt armored electric cable were installed; and a 4- by 5-foot waste chute. A single-deck cage was used to hoist men and supplies. It was operated by a single-drum hoist on the station, powered by a 60-horsepower electric motor. Four levels were run at 50-foot intervals on the south side of the raise, and one on the north side under the ore body. These levels were run from edge to edge of the ore body and were about 400 feet long. Entry crosscuts 50 to 200 feet long were run in waste to the ore, and 65-degree incline raises 6 by 6 feet in section, spaced at 60 foot intervals, were run through the ore.

Four untimbered ore passes, 6 by 9 feet in section, spaced 100 to 150 feet apart, were run from the haulage level to the crosscuts. The ore passes were covered at the top by a 90-pound grizzly with rails spaced at 12 inches. The loading chutes at the haulage level were lined with steel sheets on 12- by 12-inch timbers, and had a slope of 40 degrees on the bottom. Steel ore gates were operated by air cylinders. The ore was loaded into Granby-type cars, capacity 80 cubic feet, and trains of 12 cars were hauled by a 6-ton storage-battery locomotive to the ore bins. The battery-charging station was cut on the south side of the haulage adit near the shaft station.

The ore body was mined by the room and pillar system, and the stopes were untimbered except for occasional stulls. About 5 percent of the ore was estimated to have been left in pillars. Holes were drilled with 3-inch automatic-feed drifters mounted on air-feed bars. Blasting was done with 40 percent ammonia gelatin detonated by fuse and caps.

Detachable bits were used with $1\frac{1}{8}$-inch round steel. The broken ore in the stopes was scraped into the inclined raises and flowed into the crosscuts where it was again scraped into the ore passes and dropped to the haulage level. The stope scrapers of 42 and 48 cubic feet capacity were operated by 20- and 30-horsepower double-drum electric hoists. The crosscut scrapers were 60 cubic feet capacity and powered by 50-horsepower double-drum electric hoists. Raises holed to the surface provided natural ventilation.

The mine was operated on two 8-hour shifts: 8 a.m. to 4:30 p.m., and 6:30 p.m. to 3 a.m., with half-hour lunch periods. Miners worked on a contract price per ton or cubic-foot basis, and contracts were for a 2-week period. In October 1944 the miners were earning an average of $12.06 per day. Housing accommodations were built at Happy Camp by the Federal Housing Bureau. Board and room cost $1.60 per day, and houses for families were rented for $27.50 to $41.00 per month, completely furnished, and including water, lights, and heat.

The milling plant was located a short distance west of the portal, and Duncan L. King, mill superintendent, was in charge. The side-dumping ore cars were dumped automatically into a wooden crib-type, 500-ton-capacity, coarse-ore bin. A $3\frac{1}{2}$- by 7-foot Utah vibrating feeder fed plus 2-inch material to a 24- by 36-inch Traylor jaw crusher set to deliver a minus 2-inch product to the No. 1 conveyor belt. A 37-inch Cutler-Hammer electro magnet was suspended over the belt to remove tramp steel. No. 1 conveyor was discharged into No. 2 conveyor which fed a 3- by 6-foot Symons rod deck screen. Material over nine-sixteenths was delivered to a 3-foot standard Symons cone crusher. The plus three-eighths minus nine-sixteenths material was fed into a 4-foot short-head Symons cone crusher. The minus three-eighths-inch material from the Symons screen was discharged into No. 5 conveyor for delivery to the fine-ore bin. The product from the cone crushers was screened on a 4- by 8-foot Symons rod deck screen. Minus three-eighths-inch material was discharged into the No. 5 conveyor belt and delivered to the fine-ore bin. Plus three-eighths-inch material was returned to the 4-foot short-head cone crusher.

The fine-ore bin had a capacity of 2000 tons of minus three-eighths-inch ore. It was loaded by a hand-operated tripper on a 160-foot horizontal conveyor belt. The flow of ore from the fine-ore bin was controlled by two size "C" Hardinge constant-weight feeders. Two No. 77 Marcy ball mills loaded with 3-inch balls were driven at $24\frac{1}{2}$ revolutions per minute by 200-horsepower motors. They were in closed circuit with two 72-inch Wemco spiral classifiers. The classifier overflow was about 20 percent solids. About 90 percent of the ore was ground to minus 200-mesh, and $1\frac{1}{2}$ pounds of lime per ton of ore was added to the ball mills, and another pound of lime per ton was added to the conditioner. Reagents 238, 242, C-3, and C-5 were used as promotors, and DuPont B-23 as a frother.

Three banks of five 56-inch Fagergren flotation cells were used. The first two banks of cells were used as roughers from which the tailings went to the waste pond; concentrates went to a Denver 6- by 6-foot conditioner before being fed to the five cleaner cells. The feed to the cleaner cells was about 12 percent solids. The concentrates were first pumped by a 2-inch Wemco sand pump to a 35- by 12-foot Dorr thickener—then by a No. 2 Dorr duplex diaphragm pump to a 6-foot, five-leaf Eimco disc filter.

The tailings from the cleaner cells were pumped by a Hydroseal sand pump to a 7-foot Callow cone; underflow was returned to the ball mills, overflow was used for pulp dilution. Water from the disc filter was pumped to the mills water tank and the concentrates containing about $9\frac{1}{2}$ percent moisture were stored in a 175-ton bin equipped with a 14-inch screw conveyor for loading conveyor buckets or trucks. An aerial tramline 3.4 miles long ran over the mountain to a terminal at Thompson Creek and eliminated about 20 miles of trucking. Each tram bucket held a cubic foot of concentrates. At the terminal, the buckets were discharged into bins holding a truck load of 10 tons each. It was about an 80-mile haul to the railroad siding at Yreka, where the trucks were discharged into a 65-ton bin. An 18-inch shuttle conveyor from this bin discharged into a box-car loader, which had a capacity of about 50 tons per hour. The concentrates were shipped to the American Smelting & Refining Company smelter at Tacoma.

About 465,000 tons of 3 percent copper ore were mined and milled at this plant between March 1943 and July 1945, when the operation ended.

The ore body is considered worked out and the mine plant, machinery, and equipment have been removed. (Brown 16, pp. 817, 825; Laizure 21, p. 531; Tucker 23, p. 8; Logan 25, p. 428; Averill 35, p. 272; O'Brien 43, p. 83; 43a, p. 329.)

Mammon group, see under *Gold*.

Polar Bear claim, in sec. 12, T. 40 N., R. 8 W., M. D., is owned by Byron Burch of Seattle, and was leased to Winters and Heath of Yreka in 1943. Small amounts of chalcopyrite occur with pyrite in serpentine. Nine men were employed retimbering an old two-compartment vertical shaft said to be 210 feet deep, and in reopening an old caved adit driven N. 85° W. for 120 feet. The property was equipped with a portable compressor, pumps, and jackhammers. A bulldozer was used to prospect the surface. The operation was short lived. Some sorted material hauled to Yreka was said to have assayed too low for shipment to a smelter. (Brown 16, p. 819; O'Brien 43a, p. 329; Aubury 05, p. 106.)

Preston Peak mine. Five patented claims in sec. 22, T. 17 N., R. 5 E., H., are owned by Edgar Wallace of Los Angeles. The property is reached by about 3 miles of trail from the road at Cyclone Gap 23 miles from Waldo, Oregon. The main adit was driven about 400 feet S. 16° W. in diorite, with crosscuts east and west at 150 feet. A winze 40 feet deep was sunk from the east crosscut, and a crosscut driven S. 30° E., 32 feet from the bottom. The winze was sunk on a quartz diorite dike which is 30 feet wide, strikes S. 36° E., and dips 80° NE. The quartz diorite includes a large amount of pyrite, but no copper minerals were recognized. It is probable that this adit was driven in search of some copper mineralization showing in the cut at the portal of a short adit lying above and southwest of the portal of the main adit.

This short adit was driven about 20 feet N. 80° W. in quartz diorite including a large amount of pyrite. In the cut to the adit about 20 feet of ore was cut, said to assay 4 percent copper. The copper minerals were chalcopyrite, bornite, and some covellite, associated with pyrite.

This property was examined by geologists of the U. S. Geological Survey and mining engineers for the Reconstruction Finance Corporation in 1942, but no development work was undertaken. (Brown 16, p. 819; Maxson 33, pp. 139, 146; Aubury 05, p. 110.)

Yellow Butte mine covers 318.14 acres of patented land in the W½ sec 25, T. 43 N., R. 4 W., M. D. It is assessed to the Lone Hill Mining Company, W. E. Hills, 845 Jefferson Court, San Mateo, California, president. The incline shaft is caved and the old workings are inaccessible, but the dump shows specimens of white quartz containing pyrite, chalcopyrite, and some molybdenite. (Brown 16, p. 820; Averill 35, pp. 273, 333; Aubury 05, p. 107; 08, p. 126.)

Gold

The production of gold in Siskiyou County reached a peak of $2,351,790 in 1941, the last full year of operation before World War II.

Rising wages, the enlistment of miners in the armed forces or defense industries, difficulties in obtaining supplies, materials, and equipment, increased taxes, and governmental restrictions made it necessary to close almost all of the gold mines early in 1942. On October 8, 1942, War Production Board Order L-208 closed the few surviving mines, and in 1943 gold production in the county dropped to $110,040.

Much of the machinery and equipment used by the dredges, such as draglines, bulldozers, carryalls, electric motors, and rubber belts, was transferred to the war industries.

Gold mining has been slow to recover since it was permitted to resume operation in July 1945. The scarcity of men and materials, high wages, and taxes have made mining costly; and the price of gold has not been raised to offset the increased costs.

Abe Lincoln No. 2 placer, located on the south side of the Klamath River in sec. 6, T. 46 N., R. 12 W., M.D., is owned by Al Livingston of Fort Goff. It was last operated in a small way in 1938. (Logan 25, p. 462; Averill 35, p. 314.)

Anna Johnson and Surprise. Two unpatented claims located in the Liberty mining district, in sec. 10, T. 39 N., R. 11 W., M.D., are owned by Alex Markon of Sawyers Bar. A crushed and brecciated quartz zone has been developed by three adits driven in an easterly direction for 98, 100, and 170 feet. A fourth adit, about 350 feet northeast and 300 feet higher, which strikes S. 10° W., penetrated a crushed quartz ledge for 100 feet. This ledge is 12 feet wide, and is said to average $10 per ton in gold.

The property is equipped with a Kroch two-stamp mill with 1500-pound stamps that drop 5 inches. The ore was crushed to 25-mesh and was run over a 4- by 6-foot copper plate. Power was had from a 1924 Dodge automobile engine. A concrete arrastra 4 feet in diameter was powered by a single-cylinder gasoline engine. Markon was working alone when the property was visited in June 1945.

Autumn mine includes four claims in sec. 2, T. 40 N., R. 9 W., M.D., 4 miles north of Callahan. It is owned by I. B. Sovey and A. E. Hughes of

Callahan. A quartz vein 16 inches wide on the contact of serpentine and porphyry strikes northeast and dips vertically. It is developed by a two-compartment vertical shaft 124 feet deep with levels at 30 and 60 feet. The vein is white quartz stained red with ochre. Sorted ore is said to have assayed from $90 to $200 per ton in free gold. The vein has been stoped on the 30-foot level for 40 feet north of the shaft. On the 60-foot level, drifting on the vein has progressed 80 feet south and 120 feet north. There is some 40 feet of water in the shaft.

Three parallel veins 1 to 18 inches wide strike east and dip south on these claims; they are said to assay up to $45 per ton. There is a gallows frame of 10- by 10-inch square timbers and a frame hoist house covered with corrugated iron at the shaft. The property has been idle in recent years.

Beaudry placer in sec. 35, T. 40 N., R. 9 W., M.D., is owned by the Angele Bazet estate, c/o Marie B. LaPorte, Administratrix, 4 Laguna Street, San Francisco, California. Alexis Bourier of Callahan operated this mine a few months in the spring of 1942. He used a No. 1 giant with a 160-foot head against a 20-foot bank of gravel above serpentine bedrock. This gravel deposit is about 100 feet higher than the present channel of Fox Creek, a tributary to the South Fork of Scott River. The property is now idle. (Brown 16, p. 844; Logan 25, p. 464; Averill 35, p. 314; Haley 23, p. 99.)

Beaver Dredging Company. Leslie G. Allen, dredgemaster and part owner, operated a dragline dredge on Beaver Creek in sec. 30, T. 47 N., R. 8 W., M.D., in the summer of 1941 on land owned by Ray Taber. Equipment included a 1201 Lima dragline powered by a Cummins Diesel-228 motor and having a 70-foot boom and a 2¼-cubic-yard Esco bucket. The Judson Pacific washing plant had six steel pontoons making a barge 35 by 42 feet, 42 inches deep. The trommel was 60 inches in diameter and 30 feet long, with 20 feet of one-half to seven-eighths inch screen. The stacker belt was 30 inches wide and 65 feet long. Water was supplied by a 10-inch United Iron Works centrifugal pump. Gold was recovered in sluice boxes fitted with Hungarian riffles. The power plant included a Caterpillar D-13000 engine and a Palmer generator. An Allis Chalmers crawler-type bulldozer was used to clear the land of trees and brush. The gravel was 9 feet deep above serpentine bedrock, and 1800 cubic yards were dug by a crew of nine men in two 9-hour shifts. The plant and equipment were moved to Indian Creek near Fort Jones in Siskiyou County after only 6 weeks of operation on Beaver Creek.

Bendl Mine. Richard Bendl owns four claims about 6 miles east of Forks of Salmon, in sec. 5, T. 39 N., R. 12 W., M.D. Water for a No. 1 giant with a 2½-inch nozzle is obtained under 140 feet of head from Big Creek. The gravel bank is 20 feet high. There are 60 feet of sluice boxes 18 inches wide fitted with block riffles. Bendl operates the property alone when sufficient water is available.

Black Bear quartz mine owns 70 acres of patented land and some 29 claims by location about 7 miles southwest of Sawyers Bar, in sec. 13, T. 39 N., R. 12 W., and secs. 7 and 18, T. 39 N., R. 11 W., M.D. The mine has been idle for many years but it has produced about $3,100,000 in gold since its discovery in 1860. The property was purchased in 1945 by the Yreka Mining Company, c/o S. F. Jackson, Yreka. (Irelan 88, pp. 620, 695; Hobson 90, p. 656; Dunn 93, pp. 424, 429, 431; Crawford 94, p. 277; 96, pp. 389, 434; Brown 16, pp. 822, 826; Hamilton 22, p. 18; Tucker 23, p. 10; Logan 25, p. 431; Averill 35, pp. 274, 315; Logan 19, pp. 85, 73, 77.)

Buzzard Hill Mine, Inc. (J. E. Merriam, Bedford Hills, New York, president, Philip M. Toleman, Happy Camp, manager), consists of twelve unpatented claims located in secs. 4 and 5, T. 15 N., R. 7 E., H., and seven claims in sec. 32, T. 15 N., R. 7 E., H., (Independence mine) which were leased in 1941 to the Merriam Mining Merger, a partnership including J. E. Merriam, J. E. Merriam, Jr., and Philip M. Toleman. In July 1941 Toleman and four men were mining and cyaniding about 30 tons of gossan ore a week. The gossan was irregular in shape but appeared to be confined to a shear zone above a massive pyrite deposit striking northeast and dipping flatly east. The ore was crushed to one-eighth inch and leached 8 days in a sodium cyanide solution. Precipitation was done in zinc boxes. An 80 percent extraction was claimed for ore assaying $17.15. The property is idle. (Logan 25, p. 428; Averill 35, p. 276.)

C & E Dredging Company (A. B. Cutler, president, 315 Corbett Building, Portland, Oregon, Hugh Williamson, manager). The dredge was located on McAdam Creek about 8 miles north of Fort Jones on land leased from W. Stevens. The operation started in May 1941 on old hydraulic tailings in sec. 30, T. 45 N., R. 8 W., M.D. Equipment included a Lima dragline with a 65-foot boom and a 2¼-cubic-yard bucket powered by a Waukesha engine. The washing plant was built on six steel pontoons making a barge 36 feet wide, 48 feet long, and 42 inches deep. The trommel was 60 inches in diameter and 36 feet long with 20 feet of three-eighths to nine-sixteenths inch perforations. The stacker belt was 30 inches wide, 50 feet long and was run 320 feet per minute. Power was obtained from a D-1300 Caterpillar engine. Gold was saved in sluices fitted with Hungarian riffles and expanded metal lath over cocoa matting. The gravel was about 24 feet deep above a hard porphyry bedrock and ran from 12 to 35 cents per cubic yard. Boulders were plentiful. Thirteen men were employed on two 9-hour shifts. Operations were suspended on December 31, 1941. The dragline, bulldozer, and much of the equipment were moved away to war industries.

California American Mining Company. A group of ten claims in sec. 31, T. 47 E., R. 6 W., M.D., is owned by the P. J. McCavick estate, c/o William McCavick, Kansas City, Missouri. Quartz stringers and narrow veins occur in a red, yellow, and brown seamed andesite. The deposit has been prospected by many shallow cuts and a few short adits and shallow shafts. The quartz carries considerable pyrite in places where it is near the contact with a tan-colored shale. There is no record of production from this property, but mapping and sampling may disclose areas that can be mined profitably.

Cal Oro Dredging Company (Gardella Dredge). This bucket-line dredge is located just east of Highway 99 north of Yreka on land owned by A. Young. It has been idle since 1940 and is assessed to the E. Tubbs Estate, c/o Bank of America, Yreka. (Averill 35, p. 282; 38, p. 114.)

Chambers Hydraulic Mine. J. A. Chambers and Associates were leasing the hydraulic mine on the Ball Ranch about 3 miles northeast of Cecilville in sec. 15, T. 38 N., R. 11 W., M.D., in February 1947. Water was brought from Taylor Creek through 1800 feet of ditch and delivered to a No. 2 and a No. 4 giant under a 165-foot head through 900 feet of 15-inch pipe. The bank is 45 feet high above a slate bedrock with about 20 feet of overburden. There are 36 feet of sluices, 24 inches wide with 36-inch sides fitted with wood block riffles. One man was employed.

Chenoweth Brothers dredge is owned by a partnership composed of Kenneth and Edward Chenoweth of Hamburg, Carroll Monroe, Edward Woodzake, and Roy Thornton. They have a dragline dredge on the south bank of the Klamath River in sec. 27, T. 46 N., R. 11 W., M.D., about 3 miles west of Hamburg on 155 acres of land leased from Mrs. E. R. Titus. Four steel pontoons make a barge 32 by 20 feet. The trommel is 50 inches in diameter, 20 feet long, and has a 16-foot length of five-eighths inch screen. It is driven by a 6-cylinder Chevrolet motor. The stacker belt is 20 inches wide, 40 feet long, and is driven by a single-cylinder Wisconsin motor. Water is supplied by a LaBoure 6-inch centrifugal pump driven by a Wisconsin gasoline engine. There are three downstream and five cross sluice boxes on each side fitted with Hungarian riffles. A 5-inch Byron-Jackson centrifugal pump powered by a 4-cylinder Buick engine pumps water from the river to the pond for the washing plant. The gravel is from 20 to 40 feet deep above a hard bedrock. It will be dug by an oil- or wood-fired steam-powered Erie dragline with a 54-foot boom and a 1¼-cubic-yard bucket. The operation was about ready to start in February 1947.

Cherry Hill mine includes fourteen quartz and two placer claims in sec. 27, T. 45 N., R. 8 W., M.D. It is owned by F. G. and Carl V. Reichman and leased to G. A. Reichman, Box 122, Yreka. On the Ironside claim, a quartz vein in greenstone averages 2 to 20 inches in width, strikes S. 15° W., and dips 83° E. It is offset from 8 to 25 feet at intervals by faults striking N. 65° W., and dipping 60° N. It is developed by four adits, the longest of which is some 450 feet. The vein averages about 10 inches in width and has been stoped 80 to 100 feet to the surface for a length of 300 feet. Compressed air is delivered by an 8- by 8-inch Sullivan compressor and the rock is drilled with mounted jackhammers and steel equipped with Timken bits.

The ore is hauled about a quarter of a mile to a five-stamp mill and crushed to 50-mesh. The gold is saved by amalgamation on plates, and concentrates are saved on a Wilfley table. The ore is said to have milled $50 in free gold, and the sulphide concentrates average about $400 per ton. Some rich specimens of free gold have been found occurring with pyrite and galena. George Reichman and four other men mined and milled about 15 tons per month in 1941. The mine and mill have electric power from the California-Oregon Power Company.

The property was subleased in 1944 to the Crystal Creek Mining Company, controlled by H. F. Lintner and A. O. Witte of Redding. Some additional development was done drifting on the vein on No. 4 adit level and at the bottom of a 25-foot winze. The Wadsworth adit, 75 feet lower, was extended S. 15° W. to 200 feet and then a crosscut was driven west to a 6-inch vein striking S. 20° W. and dipping 45° E. The vein was followed a short distance south but the raise to connect with the Ironside adit was not run. The mine is idle. (Brown 16, p. 829; Logan 25, p. 436; Averill 31, p. 31; 35, pp. 276, 316.)

China Point placer in secs. 5, 6, 7, and 8, T. 16 N., R. 8 E., M.D., is owned by C. E. Regan of Happy Camp. It was operated on a small scale for a short period in the spring of 1942. Idle. (Averill 35, pp. 277, 316.)

Classic Hill mine holds some 1500 acres, of which about a third are patented, in sec. 36, T. 18 N., R. 6 E., H. It is owned by C. Scott Greening, c/o C. D. Wason, Happy Camp. In May 1937 the Happy Camp Placers, Incorporated, J. P. Morgan, president, 1003 Joshua Green

Building, Seattle, Washington, were operating the property. Water was obtained by 3½ miles of ditch from the west fork of Indian Creek and from Tom Grey Creek. It was delivered under 260-foot head to two No. 2 giants with 4½-inch nozzles. Four men were employed under A. C. Hahn, general manager, Happy Camp. The operation was short and no production was reported. (Crawford 96, p. 394; Brown 16, pp. 825, 846; Logan 25, p. 466; Averill 34, p. 306; 35, pp. 277, 316, 333.)

Conzetti quartz mine, on the upper South Fork of the Salmon River above Cecilville is owned by Ace Mills and leased with an option to purchase to J. A. Chambers and associates of Cecilville. An 18- to 28-inch quartz vein has been developed by several short cuts and adits. The outcrop was being stripped with a bulldozer in February 1947 so the vein could be sampled for possible development and mining. (Tucker 23, p. 10.)

Corbett gold (*Trust Buster mine*) includes two quartz and one placer claim and mill site in secs. 3 and 10, T. 47 N., R. 8 W., M.D. It is owned by J. L. Corbett of Hilt, California. Number 4 adit, at an elevation of 4100 feet, was driven N. 10° E. for 1500 feet. At 1200 feet a quartz vein 3½ feet wide, with granodiorite walls, dips vertically. A vein 5 feet wide at 1275 feet dips 55° N. This adit level is some 565 feet below the apex of the vein. An adit at a higher elevation is said to have been driven for 500 feet along the granodiorite hanging wall of the vein, which had a width of 8 to 10 feet and averaged $7.50 in sulphides. Equipment included a 10- by 8-inch Ingersoll-Rand portable compressor and mounted air drills. A cyanide test is said to have recovered 97 percent of gold on ore crushed to 60-mesh. The property is idle. (Averill 35, pp. 261, 317.)

Crouch mine, owned by Everett and Frances A. Crouch, consists of the Jacque Girl, Derby quartz claims, and the Log Cabin placer claim, in the Humbug Creek district. Three quartz veins from 12 to 36 inches wide are developed by a single-compartment shaft 80 feet deep, and an adit 130 feet long. In 1946 the claims were leased to A. O. Witte of Redding with an option to purchase.

Crumpton placer consists of 240 acres of patented land in sec. 2, T. 16 N., R. 7 E., H., owned by Leonard, Cliff, and Jack Crumpton of Happy Camp. Water is brought from Ranch Creek through about a mile of ditch to a reservoir and delivered to the giants through 1500 feet of steel pipe under a 200-foot head. There are 900 feet of sluice boxes 18 inches wide and 2 feet deep fitted with block riffles. The bank is about 70 feet high with about 30 feet of red soil overburden above a black schist bedrock. A great quantity of the bank has slid down into the gravel pit. The property was idle but equipped to operate in November 1946. (Averill 35, pp. 275, 317.)

Crystal Creek Mining Company, see Cherry Hill mine.

Curran Mine. E. J. Curran owns 120 acres on the south side of the North Fork of Salmon River about 2 miles below Sawyers Bar. A high channel some 60 feet above the river has about 20 feet of gravel above a clay and sepentine bedrock. Water under a 180-foot head is brought from Jessup Gulch through half a mile of ditch, and 1100 feet of flume. Gravel is washed with a No. 2 giant and the gold is recovered in 300 feet of sluice boxes 18 inches wide and 2 feet high, fitted with 8-inch block riffles. Curran was working alone and moving about 60 yards per day in the 1941 season.

Dania Mine. Larsen Brothers and Harms Brothers, Route 4, Box 2220, Sacramento, California, operated a dragline dredge on the Klamath River in sec. 7, T. 46 N., R. 7 W., M.D., on ground included in the Clyburn placer. Equipment included a 5-cubic-yard Marion-Walker dragline with a 100-foot boom, and powered with a 300-horsepower Fairbanks-Morse engine. The boat was built by Hickinboatham Brothers of Stockton and was made of seven steel pontoons covering an area 8 feet by 36 feet, and had an additional 4 feet added to each side to make a barge 64 by 36 feet in area. The washing plant had a trommel 60 inches in diameter, and was 40 feet long with a 30-foot length of one-half to three-eighths inch screen. Water was supplied by a Byron-Jackson 10-inch centrifugal pump. The stacker belt was 36 inches wide and 100 feet long. Power was furnished by a D-17000 Caterpillar diesel. Hungarian riffles with mercury traps were used to save the gold. The gravel was about 35 feet deep, and about 4000 cubic yards per day was being dug in July 1941. Twelve men were employed on three shifts under R. J. Barrett, dredgemaster. This operation was closed down and much of its equipment moved to war industries in the summer of 1942.

Donnelly placer holds 40 acres in sec. 7, T. 16 N., R. 8 E., H., on the west bank of the Klamath River. It is owned by C. E. Reagan of Happy Camp. A gravel bench about 25 feet above the river is about 300 feet wide, and gravel is 14 to 60 feet deep above a greenstone bedrock. A Byron-Jackson 8-inch centrifugal pump driven by a 6-cylinder Fageol gasoline engine, coupled with a 4-cylinder Waukesha gasoline engine, furnished water for a No. 2 giant. Wash water was supplied by a Worthington 12-inch centrifugal pump. There were 60 feet of 2- by 2½-foot sluice boxes fitted with block riffles. Test pits are said to have indicated an average of 25 cents per yard for the gravel. The property was under lease to the Hillside Gold Company and sub-leased to the Joyce Gold Company, Joyce Hittson, Box 351, Huntington Beach, California, in November 1946. It was idle when visited November 14, 1946.

Eliza group of four claims and mill site in secs. 4, 5, 8, and 9, T. 45 N., R. 8 W., M.D., is owned by the DeWitt and Lawson Estate of Yreka and is leased to the Gold Crown Mining and Milling Company, Seattle, Washington. W. H. Price of Yreka is vice-president and general manager. The mine plant at the portal of No. 5 adit includes an Ingersoll-Rand 10- by 12-inch compressor geared to an 8-cylinder automobile engine, a Gardner-Denver portable compressor Model 9xJ20, 2 Sullivan stopers, a Sullivan drifter, and accessory equipment sufficient to develop and mine on a small scale. The milling plant included a 6- by 6-inch Blake crusher, a 40- by 40-inch Marcy ball mill, screen classifier, Mineral Separation jig, and five Mineral Separation flotation cells. Power is furnished by a variety of gasoline and diesel engines. Water flows to the mill from springs on the hill above.

The No. 5 adit was driven S. 10° W. for 260 feet, where it cut a 3-foot quartz vein striking S. 18° W. and dipping 78° W., with black fault gouge on both walls. The vein is laminated and stained brown and black. Throughout several hundred feet of drifting the vein has showed few changes in width and only minor offsets from faulting. A former operator estimated that it would average $5 in gold per ton. The fourth level is said to be 137 feet vertically above No. 5, and no stoping has been done between levels. The free-milling portion of the vein above No. 4 level has been stoped and is said to have yielded $150,000 when treated by amalgamation in a 10-stamp mill. No new development work has been done on this property, aside from assessment work, in recent years. (Brown 16, p. 831; Tucker 22, p. 297; 22a, p. 600; 23, p. 11; 23a, p. 138; Logan 25, p. 439; Averill 31, p. 32; 35, pp. 280, 318.)

Enterprise placer at Scott Bar in sec. 21, T. 45 N., R. 10 W., M.D., is owned by Hollis Anderson and associates of Scott Bar. It includes portions of an ancient channel of the Scott River high above its present level. It was worked as a drift mine from an adit said to be 1000 feet long in 1888. No new work has been done at this property in recent years. (Crawford 96, p. 399; Logan 25, p. 439; Averill 35, p. 281.)

Etna Gold Dredging Company is controlled by William A. Kettlewell and W. S. Mead, 1730 Franklin Street, Oakland, California. A Walter Johnson bucket-line dredge was operated on Wildcat Creek about 2 miles northwest of Callahan in sec. 13, T. 40 N., R. 9 W., M.D., from December 1939 to December 1941. The dredge was built on 19 steel pontoons, making a hull 36 by 80 feet. The digging ladder was 60 feet long, and the chain of 79 3-cubic-foot buckets was driven by a 75-horsepower electric motor. The trommel was 54 inches in diameter and 25 feet long, with 19 feet of three-eighths to 1-inch holes, and was rotated by a 15-horsepower motor. The stacker belt was 24 inches wide and 70 feet long between pulleys. It was operated by a 15-horsepower electric motor. There were five cross sluices 29 inches wide by 14 feet long discharging into two downstream sluices, 36 inches wide and 24 and 30 feet long, fitted with Hungarian riffles on each side. There were mercury traps under the cross sluices. Water was pumped with a Byron-Jackson 10-inch centrifugal pump driven by a 60-horsepower electric motor. A 3-inch centrifugal pump driven by a 10-horsepower motor supplied water for the clean-up and for fire protection. The Johnson winch was operated by a 25-horsepower General Electric motor. The friction brakes had an automatic air-control device to set them in case of power failure. Boulders over 20 inches in size were by-passed to starboard before entering the trommel, and there were two rock chutes at the stern to discard rocks before they reached the stacker belt. The gravel was from 8½ to 27 feet deep above a hard slate and serpentine bedrock. The dredge was digging about 2000 cubic yards in 24 hours in July 1941. Fifteen men were employed under Oscar Bahrenburg, dredgemaster. This dredge was dismantled for shipment to Alaska early in 1942.

Farnsworth hydraulic mine on the South Fork of Salmon River in the Cecilville district includes two association placer claims of 160 acres each, and two 20-acre placer claims. It is owned by Edward McBroom of Cecilville. Water is obtained from the South Fork of Salmon River through 5 miles of ditch. It is delivered to a giant with a 6-inch nozzle under a 120-foot head. The bank is about 40 feet high with 6 to 8 feet of gravel above a gray andesite bedrock. Gold is recovered in three lengths of sluice boxes 3 feet wide with railroad-iron riffles. McBroom and Kenneth Kinsman operated the property as partners in the 1947 season.

Fort Goff hydraulic mine in sec. 31, T. 47 N., R. 12 W., M. D., includes 80 acres of patented land on the north bank of the Klamath River, owned by Frank Schulmeyer. The property has been idle for many years but J. W. Welch of Seiad had five men employed in February 1947 repairing the 1½ miles of ditch and flume from Fort Goff Creek preparing to operate. (Irelan 88, p. 596; Crawford 94, p. 282; 96, p. 401; Brown 16, p. 850; Averill 35, p. 319.)

French Gulch Gold Dredging Company, 2404 Russ Building, San Francisco, closed their operation on Clear Creek in Shasta County in July 1946 and moved the dredge and equipment to Indian Creek in Siskiyou County near Fort Jones on land situated in secs. 13 and 14, T. 44 N., R. 9 W., M. D., owned by George Milne of Fort Jones. The bucket-ladder dredge was built by the Washington Iron Works of Seattle in 1940. It has a pontoon-type hull 90 by 40 feet and 7 feet deep. The 85-foot digging ladder carries 75 buckets of $4\frac{1}{2}$ cubic feet capacity. The trommel is 5 feet in diameter and has a 21-foot length of slotted screen with three-eighths inch holes spaced at $1\frac{1}{2}$- and 1-inch intervals. There are eight 30-inch sluices 10 feet long feeding two 30-inch downstream sluices fitted with rubber Hungarian riffles on each side. Two Bingham centrifugal pumps, an 8-inch and a 10-inch, supply the water. All equipment is operated by electric motors. The gravel is about 18 feet deep on Indian Creek. Etheredge Walker, 2404 Russ Building, San Francisco, is president of the company; Ed Shuford is dredgemaster at Indian Creek. Eighteen men are employed.

Gibralter mine, 81 acres of patented ground in sec. 13, T. 43 N., R. 10 W., M. D., is owned by the C. E. Jacobsen Estate, Greenville. A quartz vein 18 to 42 inches wide strikes N. 5° E. and dips 34° E. It is developed by an incline shaft on the vein for a depth of 100 feet. At 90 feet depth, a drift was run north on the vein for 60 feet, and a raise was run up 18 feet above the drift at 20 feet north of the shaft. The vein was about 20 inches wide and is said to have yielded 35 tons of ore assaying $28.50 per ton in gold. The property was equipped with a single drum hoist geared to a four-cylinder gasoline engine. Compressed air was delivered by a Schram 7- by 9-inch compressor driven by a Sterling gasoline engine.

The mill was equipped with an ore bin topped with a bar grizzly spaced at $1\frac{1}{4}$ inches; a Challenge ore feeder; Pacific Iron Works five-stamp mill with a 10-mesh screen; and a 4- by 12-inch copper lip plate followed by a 4- by 4-foot copper amalgamating plate. The tailing was ground to 50-mesh in a Straub ball mill and treated in a Gibson impact amalgamator. The tailing from the amalgamator was treated in four Denver flotation cells and finally on a Deister table. A Dorr rake classifier was cut out of the circuit. The laboratory was equipped with a Braun "chipmunk" crusher and a Braun disc pulverizer. All mill equipment was driven by electric motors. Water was pumped from a shaft in the valley by a Fairbanks-Morse centrifugal pump through 600 feet of 2-inch line against a 125-foot head. The pump was driven by a $7\frac{1}{2}$-horsepower electric motor. This property has been idle since May 1941.

Gold Bar mine includes 12 unpatented claims about a mile north of Hawkinsville in sec. 2, T. 45 N., R. 7 W., M. D. It is owned by D. G. Thompson of Yreka. Quartz stringers and narrow veins in meta-andesite have been developed by four shafts up to 50 feet in depth, five adits up to 140 feet in length, and numerous shallow pits and trenches. Thompson claimed that composite samples of the meta-andesite in zones including quartz stringers, indicate that an average of $4 to $5 per ton in gold can be mined from a large area on the surface. The property is equipped with a Chicago pneumatic portable air compressor, a mounted rock drill, rubber-tired wheel barrow, and small tools. It was idle when visited in March 1947.

Gold Mountain group includes 29 claims in sec. 2, T. 41 N., R. 7 W., and sec. 35, T. 42 N., R. 7 W., M. D., owned by James and Agnes Furlong of San Francisco and Arvil V. Miner of Richmond. Numerous outcrops of quartz, quartz diorite porphyry, and quartzite occur near the contact of Paleozoic sediments with serpentine and diorite. In some places they carry considerable pyrite and some pyrrhotite. They have been prospected by numerous cuts and trenches and two adits. The north adit was run in a S. 47° W. direction for about 235 feet through diorite containing pyrite and some pyrrhotite. It was said to assay from $1 to $2 per ton in gold and to show a trace of nickel.

The east adit was driven S. 15° E. for 215 feet in quartz diorite which bore considerable pyrite. There are several zones of quartzite in which are seams of white quartz striking east. One zone 40 feet wide outcrops 15 feet above the ground and strikes S. 60° E. The southwest adit was run N. 20° W. for 90 feet through gray quartz diorite having seams of red iron oxide. This material was said to assay from $2 to $7 per ton in gold. The south adit, said to have been started in 1876, was driven in a northwesterly direction for some 500 feet through a pyrite-bearing gray quartz diorite with narrow quartz seams. No assays were reported from this adit. The claims have been idle except for assessment work in recent years. Mapping and sampling might disclose zones where low-grade gold ores could be mined profitably.

Gold Reef mine includes 280 acres of patented land in sec. 34, T. 43 N., R. 10 W., M. D., owned by the John F. Lewis Estate, Fort Jones. It was leased to Philip Suetter of Portland in 1941-42 with an option to purchase. A crosscut run S. 83° W. for 215 feet cut 25 feet of pyrite near the face which assayed $2 per ton in gold but contained no copper. About 85 feet above the crosscut, a leached white sugary quartz, stained yellow, brown, and black in streaks, outcrops for a width of about 21 feet for a length of about 500 feet in a S. 25° W. direction. It was said to assay $4.50 per ton in gold. Both walls are meta-andesite. The outcrop was stripped of 15 feet of overburden with an International T-D9 bulldozer. Vertical holes were drilled 5 feet deep, spaced at about 3-foot intervals, and blasted to make a trench 15 feet wide. The ore was loaded into mine cars with a link-belt "Speedster L-S40" shovel, and hauled to a 20-ton bin by a Ford model "A" powered locomotive. It was crushed to minus 2-inch size in a 20-inch gyratory crusher. A three-rail, 24-inch gauge tramline, built of 24-pound rails on a 32 percent grade for a length of 1420 feet had two three-fourths-ton cars which dumped automatically into the 20-ton mill ore bin. Ore was crushed to 40-mesh in two "Clyde Smith" ball mills and was treated in two Cascade amalgamators and on five Wilfley tables. An experimental 20-ton copper smelter was purchased to treat the concentrates. The mill treated 30 tons per day for about 3 months in 1942, then all operations were shut down. This property was fully and completely equipped and was provided with bunk and boarding houses, offices, laboratories, electric-light plant, and water system. It has since been dismantled.

Gold Ventures Ltd., Paul A. Bundy, president and general manager, Box 323, Grass Valley, California, have a lease with an option to purchase on the Portuguese placer mine in sec. 4, T. 46 N., R. 12 W., and sec. 32, T. 47 N., R. 12 W., M. D., from Stanly Davis of San Francisco, California. They are assembling a dragline dredge on the property. Equipment includes a Lima dragline with a 70-foot boom and a 3-cubic-yard bucket. It is powered by a Cummins 250-horsepower diesel engine. The Bodinson washing plant has five steel pontoons making a hull 36 by 48 feet and 54 inches deep. The trommel is 60 inches in diameter and 39 feet long, with 25 feet of half-inch holes. The stacker belt is 36 inches wide and 70 feet long between pulleys. There are 10 side sluices 30 inches wide and two downstream sluices 30 inches wide fitted with Hungarian riffles on each side. Water will be furnished by a 10- and a 4-inch United Iron Works centrifugal pump. Power will be supplied by a 200-horsepower Murphy diesel-electric motor and each piece of equipment will have a separate motor drive. There is an International T-D-18 bulldozer for clearing the land, and a Rowe 300-ampere arc welder to make necessary repairs to steel equipment. Ten men were employed May 28, 1947 under John Frasher. This dredge was moved from Bridgeport and was formerly known as the Sunmar dredge.

Golden Eagle mine is on patented land in sec. 11, T. 44 N., R. 9 W., M.D., owned by George Milne of Fort Jones. It has had an estimated production of $1,000,000 but has been idle since 1931. (Irelan 88, p. 625; Crawford 94, p. 282; Logan 25, p. 440; Averill 31, p. 35; 35, pp. 283, 319.)

Golden Rule mine includes three quartz claims and a mill site on the North Fork of Hungry Creek in sec. 26, T. 48 N., R. 8 W., M.D. It is owned by Robert Claye Jr. of Yreka, who purchased it from R. T. Baldwin in 1938. An 8- to 10-inch quartz vein in granodiorite strikes S. 85° E. and dips 87° N. It is developed by a 4- to 6-foot shaft 20 feet deep and a drift run S. 85° E. for 20 feet. There is a single-drum hoist with a Fairbanks-Morse gasoline engine to hoist a bucket made from a gasoline drum. An old shaft 65 feet deep was filled with waste rock from the new shaft. An adit whose portal is about 80 feet east of the shaft and 90 feet lower, was driven about 300 feet with 100 feet of drift on the vein. The ore was milled in a 5-ton Chilean mill, belt driven by a 4-horsepower gasoline engine, and the gold was recovered by amalgamation and concentration on an Ellis table. Some pyrite and chalcopyrite is associated with the quartz. Robert Claye and his son work alone at this property. (Averill 35, pp. 261, 319.)

Golden Wonder group of six quartz and two placer claims in Timber Gulch, in secs. 27, 28, and 34, T. 45 N., R. 8 W., M.D., is owned by Fred Talbott. This property has been idle except for occasional small-scale ground sluicing by Talbott. Water is obtained from a reservoir through 300 feet of 6-inch pipe, and is delivered to a giant with a 2-inch nozzle under a 50-foot head.

Hansen group, includes the Hansen, Gilta, Gold Run, and Knownothing claims on Knownothing Creek in secs. 1 and 12, T. 9 N., R. 7 E. It is owned by Bessie M. Hansen and Marian Justus of Forks of Salmon. Norman Marvin of Etna is reported to have recovered 100 ounces of gold from 30 tons of sorted ore on this property in 1946. (Dunn 93, p. 446; Crawford 94, p. 284; 96, p. 404; Logan 25, p. 442; Averill 35, p. 285.)

Hegler (Oregon) mine includes a group of claims in Lawson Gulch in sec. 3, T. 45 N., R. 8 W., M.D., owned by H. L. Heinrichsen and Nick G. Kapranos of Yreka. It was leased in 1947 to Max Erwin of Yreka who had three men employed reopening an old adit that was caved near the portal. The property was last worked in 1917 and is said to have a vein 2 to 6 feet wide that averaged $5 a ton in free gold. (Dunn 93, p. 446; Crawford 94, p. 284; 96, p. 405; Logan 25, p. 453; Averill 35, p. 325.)

Hogan mine is a group of six claims in sec. 32, T. 41 N., R. 10 W., M.D., owned by George Baker of Etna. A quartz vein 6 to 12 inches wide with granodiorite walls strikes S. 20° E. and dips 28° E. It is developed by several short adits and surface cuts. A portion of the vein has been stoped to the surface. There is a one-stamp mill equipped with two 30- by 48-inch copper amalgamating plates and an 8-inch sluice box 6 feet long fitted with expanded metal over burlap. The mill can be run by 36-inch Pelton water wheel when there is sufficient water, and it has a one-cylinder Novo gas engine as auxiliary power. Baker said he purchased this property from James O'Connell in 1935 and he has been working alone, mining and milling about 25 tons per year. (Averill 35, pp. 302, 321.)

Homestead placer claim, located in sec. 2, T. 40 N., R. 9 W., M.D., is owned by A. E. Hughes of Etna. The gravel is from 2 to 8 feet deep above andesite and serpentine bedrock. Water is brought from Sugar Creek through 9 miles of ditch and about 300 feet of 6- and 7-inch pipe to a giant, under a 50-foot head. A "self shooter" installed in a 24- by 24-inch flume 30 feet long is used when water is low. Gold is recovered in 60 feet of bedrock race and 32 feet of sluice boxes 24 inches wide and 12 inches deep. Hughes and George Cory operate the property as partners.

Horton Gulch. A group of 200 acres held by location, and the adjoining Mount Shasta Mining Company property of 131 acres of patented land, in secs. 29 and 30, T. 38 N., R. 11 W., M.D., are owned by John D. and Ada McBroom of Cecilville. Portions of these properties were worked by hydraulic mining, but they have been idle in recent years. They were leased to William I. Zoch in 1945 and were being considered for possible dredging. (Averill 46, p. 294.)

Humming Bug Mine, Inc., C. S. Haley, president, owns 620 acres of land in sec. 17, T. 45 N., R. 7 W., M.D. A $3\frac{1}{2}$-foot quartz vein carrying gold is developed by a 700-foot adit. The property has been idle since 1939 when fire destroyed the compressor, drill sharpener, and several rock drills. Much of the machinery for the 40-ton flotation mill has been sold and removed.

Ida May mine, in sec. 15, T. 39 N., R. 11 W., M.D., was last operated by the Norcal Mining Company in 1938. The Ida May, Francis Bell, and Lucky Strike claims have since been purchased from the Norcal Company by John W. Usher of Sawyers Bar. Usher has been sluicing the Ida May dump through 40 feet of 12- by 12-inch sluice boxes fitted with metal-lath riffles. Water is obtained from Eddy Creek. He has combined the three Ida May claims with four adjoining claims to form the *Security Mines group*. (Tucker 22, p. 297; 23, p. 11; Logan 25, p. 445; Averill 35, pp. 301, 321.)

Indian Bottoms Mining Company, 356 South Mission Road, Los Angeles, California, owns four claims and leases one claim on the north bank of the Salmon River in secs. 16, 20, and 21, T. 11 N., R. 7 E., H. An old river channel some 40 feet higher than the present river has a bank about 40 feet high, including a gravel bed about 7 feet thick above granite bedrock. Water is obtained from Portuguese Creek and delivered under a head of 126 feet to two No. 4 giants fitted with 6-inch nozzles. Gold is recovered in 360 feet of 30- by 30-inch sluice boxes fitted with steel rails for the first 24 feet, and then with 9-inch block riffles. The boxes drop 8 inches in 12 feet. A derrick for handling boulders has a mast 86 feet high and a boom 90 feet long. It is equipped with a 65-horsepower Caterpillar diesel engine. A Palmer 25-kilowatt generator driven by 75-horse-power International diesel engine provides electricity for the flood lights and camp buildings. Six men were employed on each of two shifts in September 1941. This property is now idle.

Joubert placer includes 90 acres of land 2 miles south of Sawyers Bar in secs. 4, 8, and 9, T. 39 N., R. 11 W., M.D., owned by L. J. Joubert of Sawyers Bar. From 1938-46, three hydraulic pits on this property were leased to Stanley Czerwinski, who had 7 men employed. Water was obtained from Eddys Gulch through about 4000 feet of flume and ditch. A small reservoir above the pits supplied water under a 180-foot head to two giants with 4-inch and 3-inch nozzles respectively. There are about 30 feet of loose gravel with 20 feet of overburden above a hard slate bedrock. About 600 feet of 18- by 30-inch sluice boxes sloping 6 inches to 12 feet are fitted with block riffles.

In 1947 the property was leased to Alex Markon and his stepsons, Gene and Melvin Cramer. They were directing water from a 3-inch nozzle against a bank 50 feet high including about 30 feet of loose gravel above a hard blue slate bedrock. They had 72 feet of sluice boxes 16 by 16 inches with a slope of 8 inches to 12 feet. Of 33.78 ounces of gold recovered, only 10 ounces could be screened through a 10-mesh screen, so they were installing an undercurrent to trap any finer gold that might be present. The Joubert placer was first operated in 1855 and it is described in earlier reports of the State Division of Mines. (Logan 25, p. 474; Averill 46, p. 294.)

Judge hydraulic mine includes six unpatented claims in sec. 33, T. 40 N., R. 11 W., M.D., owned by J. F. and Patricia Judge of Santa Monica, California. It is leased to a copartnership including H. D. Winship, Vernon Allen, and E. A. Von Gerlitz. About 1½ miles of ditch provides water under a 200-foot head from Eddys Gulch. In March 1947 two men were employed using a No. 2 giant with a 4-inch nozzle. The bank was about 100 feet high including loose red soil and 50 feet of gravel above a hard slate bedrock. There are about 500 feet of 2- by 2-foot sluice boxes lined with rail and block riffles. A derrick for handling boulders has a 70-foot mast and is powered with a single-drum hoist geared to a 1-cylinder gasoline engine. The bank is said to run from 35 cents to $1 per cubic yard.

Kanaka Hill hydraulic mine includes eight 20-acre claims on the east bank of the Klamath River in secs. 27, 28, and 34, T. 16 N., R. 7 E., H., owned by Steve S. Green of Happy Camp. Two old river terraces 50 and 185 feet above the present river are estimated to contain 1,200,000 yards of gravel above a greenstone-schist bedrock that will average 20 cents per cubic yard in gold. Water is available from Kanaka Creek through two ditches delivering water to either the upper or lower gravel under 140 feet of head. Additional water can be obtained from Wilson and Buzzard Creeks by digging the necessary ditches. The property has not been operated for several years, and the ditches, pipe lines, and sluice boxes will need some repairs. (Averill 35, pp. 290, 321.)

K. C. mine includes 10 mining claims, one of which is patented, in sec. 6, T. 45 N., R. 9 W., and all of sec. 1, T. 45 N., R. 10 W., M.D., except Lot 1, owned by Florence M. Cooper, Yreka. It is leased with an option to purchase by A. L. Damon, president of the Thompson Divide Mining Company. A quartz vein 8 to 48 inches wide strikes S. 30° to 70° W. and dips 18° to 33° N. The quartz is stained brown and is in bands from 1½ to 4 inches wide separated by thin layers of black broken shale with light-brown clay seams. The property is developed by five adits from 80 to 400 feet long, three of which are caved and inaccessible, by short raises on the vein, and by open cuts on the vein. The vein in No. 2 adit is said to have been 2.2 feet wide and to have averaged $18.75 per ton in free gold. Both walls are black shale. A new mill building has been built at the camp site from lumber sawed on the property. Dump trucks will haul the ore $1\frac{1}{4}$ miles down hill to the mill and discharge over a rail grizzly with three-fourths-inch spaces and sloping 45°. The undersize will fall into the fine-ore bin. Oversize will be crushed to half an inch in a 6- by 8-inch jaw crusher, and discharged into the fine-ore bin. The fine-ore bin has two chutes from which the ore is drawn by disc feeders to feed a 2- and a 5-stamp battery. The stamps weigh 1250 pounds and will drop 6 inches, 100 times per minute. The ore will be crushed to minus 40-mesh and amalgamated on copper plates. The tailing will be concentrated on a Wilfley table. It is expected that 25 tons in 24 hours will be milled. Water is obtained by gravity from a spring and delivered through 1000 feet of 2-inch pipe to a 1200-gallon-capacity galvanized-iron tank. Power will be obtained from a diesel engine which has not yet been delivered. There are five cabins including a boarding house at the camp. Seven men and a cook were employed May 28, 1947 under Tom Clark, superintendent. (Averill 31, p. 35; 35, p. 321.)

Katie May group of five claims in secs. 13 and 24, T. 45 N., R. 8 W., M.D., is owned by A. S. and Frances E. Calkins. Quartz stringers and narrow veins 4 to 14 inches wide occur in greenstone near a contact with black shale. They have been prospected by numerous surface cuts, several short adits and shallow shafts, most of which are now caved. Averill (35, p. 291) quotes a former lessee as saying that $70,000 was produced from a 10-inch vein in a stope 40 feet long. In October 1945, A. O. Witte of Redding, California, leased and prospected this property, but no operation ensued. (Crawford 96, p. 409; Brown 16, p. 836; Logan 25, p. 448; Averill 35, pp. 291, 308, 321.)

Keenan mine comprises 40 acres of patented land in the $NE\frac{1}{4}$ sec. 7, T. 43 N., R. 9 W., M.D., and one unpatented claim in sec. 12, T. 43 N., R. 10 W., M.D., owned by Arthur Keenan, Fort Jones. A quartz vein $3\frac{1}{2}$ feet wide strikes N. 10° E. and dips 45° E. It is developed by a shaft 111 feet deep on the vein, and a crosscut to the vein from a point 100 feet south and 50 feet lower. A second adit, 175 feet lower than the collar of the shaft and 300 feet south was driven 300 feet to a fault striking N. 60° E. and dipping steeply southeast. Seventy feet of drifting along the fault did not pick up the vein. The mine is idle and the shaft is almost full of water.

King Solomon mine on Mathews Creek in sec 14, T. 38 N., R. 12 W., M.D., includes 12 claims owned by George Milne of Fort Jones. It was last operated by the King Solomon Mines Company in October 1940. Machinery and equipment have since been removed. The mill tailing was reworked by William George of Sawyers Bar and Virgil Gray of Cecilville in 1945 and 1946. Water from Mathews Creek was diverted against the tailing to wash it into about 120 feet of sluice boxes fitted with Hungarian riffles. Coarse material was screened out at the first box. Water from a fire hose fitted with a $1\frac{1}{4}$-inch nozzle helped to move the material. The mill tailing has been practically all cleaned up. (Jenkins 35, p. 159; Averill 35, p. 321.)

Klamath River dredge was operated by the Wm. von der Hellen Mining Company, Box 1026, Medford, Oregon. The company owns a strip of land 400 feet wide along the Klamath River in sec. 16, T. 46 N., R. 7 W., M.D. Operations started in July 1940 with new equipment including a three-winch Monighan dragline with an 80-foot boom, and a 2½-cubic-yard bucket. It had a Fairbanks diesel engine rated at 190 horsepower. The washing plant was built by Hickinboatham Brothers of Stockton and had six steel pontoons, making a barge 48 by 36 feet; and a trommel 64 inches in diameter, 35 feet long, with 24 feet of three-eighths- to five-eighths-inch holes. The stacker belt was 36 inches wide and 70 feet long. Water was supplied by a United Iron Works 10-inch centrifugal pump. Gold was recovered in sluice boxes fitted with steel Hungarian riffles. Power was furnished by a Caterpillar D-13000 engine. The gravel was 28 feet deep above a hard bedrock and a crew of 12 men was digging 2500 cubic yards in three shifts. Sands were treated in a cleanup barrel 30 inches in diameter by 3½ feet long, by rotating 300 pounds of sands and 2 pounds of mercury with eight 6-inch manganese-steel blocks to polish the gold. The dredge was shut down September 27, 1942, and much of the equipment moved to war industries. It has not been operated since.

Last Chance mine consists of three claims in the SE¼ sec. 23, T. 48 N., R. 8 W., M.D., owned and operated by a co-partnership composed of Stuart Cosgrave, A. A. Carlson, and John Krallman, Box 624, Yreka. The property was purchased in 1945 from Gus and George Avergis, who had sunk a vertical shaft 18 feet deep on a 20-inch quartz vein striking N. 87° W. in granodiorite. The new owners sank a new shaft about 15 feet east on a 45° E. incline 80 feet deep, but did not find the vein until they cross-cut west for 18 feet at a depth of 60 feet. The quartz was only 2½ inches wide at this depth, but it was said to assay $152 per ton. A single-drum Smith and Western hoist driven by a Milwaukee air-cooled gasoline engine pulls a mine-car skip up the shaft to dump into a wooden bin. An Ingersoll Rand compressor, belt-driven by a Star automobile engine provides compressed air for drilling. Mill equipment includes a 10- by 14-inch jaw crusher, belt-driven by an old automobile engine; a 50-ton-capacity Hardinge ball mill, belt-driven by G.M.C. engine; a Dorr double-rake classifier; and a five-plate cascade amalgamator. The ball mill and classifier were not used and the cascade amalgamator was to be replaced by a 5-ton Huntington mill. Water is obtained from a spring and flows through a 1-inch pipeline to a 12- by 16- by 6-foot concrete tank. Three frame cabins, a bunkhouse, boardinghouse, and tents are provided for the employees. The property was idle when visited in August 1946.

Lincoln Gold Dredging Company, a partnership of E. M. (Bing) Clark, Redding, California, and W. K. Jansen, Lincoln, California, operated a dragline dredge on Greenhorn Creek about 2 miles west of Highway 99 in sec. 29, T. 45 N., R. 7 W., M.D. The equipment was moved from the Trinity River near Lewiston and started operating at this location July 10, 1941. It included a P & H dragline with a 60-foot boom using a 1¾-cubic-yard bucket and powered by a D-13000 Caterpillar engine. The washing plant was built on five steel pontoons, 8 by 30 by 3 feet, making a hull 40 by 30 feet. The trommel was 54 inches in diameter and 28 feet long with 18 feet of three-eighths- to 1½-inch holes. The stacker belt was 36 inches wide and 50 feet long. Power was obtained from a D-13000 Caterpillar engine, and a General Electric generator supplied current for lights. The sluice boxes were 28 inches wide and there were eight cross sluices and three downstream sluices on each side. The cross sluices were fitted with Hungarian riffles and the downstream sluices had expanded metal over cocoa matting, and a 12- by 28-inch copper amalgamating plate under the expanded metal in each sluice. Water was pumped by a 6-inch centrifugal pump driven by a D4 Caterpillar engine. The gravel was 16 feet deep over a fairly hard slate bedrock. In July 1941 the operators were digging about 2000 yards of gravel in 24 hours, which yielded about 18 cents per cubic yard.

Three men were employed on each of three shifts, and an extra man on day shift to operate the D6 Caterpillar bulldozer clearing the brush and overburden from the gravel. E. M. Clark was in charge of operations.

Long Gulch mine in sec 8, T. 45 N., R. 7 W., M.D., includes the Gold Leaf, Beauty, and Prairie claims owned by Paul and Harry C. Dobyns, 227 Pine Street, Yreka, California. It is leased, with an option to purchase, by a co-partnership composed of A. N. Whealdon, E. L. McNaughton, G. Ankeney, and H. F. Lintner of Redding. A quartz vein averaging about 3 feet in width has been developed by three adits. The lowest adit is about 450 feet long, 350 feet of which is a drift on a vein 2 to 3½ feet wide striking S. 35° W. to S. 72° W., and dipping 45° to 67° NW. At about 160 feet from the portal, a 40-foot raise on the vein holed to surface, and at 430 feet a second raise was run to connect with the adit level 70 feet above. It holed into the adit about 20 feet from the face. The vein averaged 30 inches in width in the raise except where faulted 16 feet to the south. The adit 70 feet higher drifted 176 feet on the vein, and a third adit 300 feet higher has a drift 55 feet long on the vein and a 40-foot raise to surface. The ore from this upper adit was milled in an 8-foot arrastra in 1914, but the recovery is not known. Recent mill tests show that there is little free gold.

The vein is white quartz with fine, sharp, pyrite cubes and occasionally some galena. The walls are greenstone with thin seams of quartz parallel to the vein, and include many fine, bright cubes of pyrite. The vein has been faulted to the south for a maximum distance of 16 feet in three places by faults striking S. 70° to 80° W. and dipping 22° to 30° S. Equipment includes a Gardner compressor driven by a four-cylinder Ford engine; a mounted rock drill; mine car, and accessory small tools. Two men are employed drifting and raising on the vein to block out sufficient ore to justify building a mill. (Crawford 96, p. 413.)

Lucky Boy mine in sec. 33, T. 17 N., R. 8 E., H., includes seven unpatented claims owned by Harry Sibley, J. W. Stanton, and Martin Jolly of Happy Camp, California. A belt of tan-colored pyritic schist with numerous quartz stringers and some narrow quartz veins has been prospected by numerous surface cuts and short adits. Twenty-three samples are said to have averaged $4.71 per ton in gold. Ore from a stope on the Lady Luck claim 100 feet long and 10 feet wide is said to average $10 per ton in gold. Another adit is said to have 4 feet of ore assaying $5.75 per ton in gold and 2½ percent copper. There is a two-room cabin on this property. No work, except prospecting has been done in recent years.

Lumgrey mine, consists of eight claims in sec. 22, T. 47 N., R. 8 W., M.D., owned by H. H. Lotz, Klamath River Post Office. A zone of quartz stringers in a granodiorite schist is said to average $5.20 per ton in gold. From 1700 tons of ore milled in 1939 in a 10-stamp mill, a 34 percent recovery by amalgamation is reported. The property is idle except for assessment work. (Averill 35, pp. 261, 322.)

Mammon group includes 17 claims in sec. 14, T. 41 N., R. 7 W., M. D., owned by James and Agnes Furlong of San Francisco and Arvil V. Miner of Richmond. Numerous outcrops of copper-stained quartz and quartz porphyry dikes occur on these claims. They are near the contact of granodiorite with shale. On the Mammon No. 4 claim, a northward-trending 18-inch quartz vein carrying some chalcopyrite is said to assay $7 per ton in gold. It was prospected by a pit 4 by 6 feet and 6 feet deep. An adit 150 feet long at a lower elevation did not reach the vein.

On Mammon No. 9, a prospect crosscut was driven S. 55° E. for 550 feet, but no vein was encountered. On Mammon No. 1, a quartz porphyry dike at the "Barrundon" cut strikes S. 65° E. and dips 64° S., and is said to assay $5.40 per ton in gold for a width of 21 feet. A 6-by 10-foot shaft 9 feet deep was sunk on a 4-foot vein striking S. 25° W. and dipping 55° to 90° E. This vein was said to assay $3\frac{1}{2}$ percent copper and $33 per ton in gold. The country rock is granodiorite.

On Mammon No. 11, a shaft 18 feet deep was filled with water and inaccessible; quartz examined on the dump was stained with copper minerals. Ore from a trench 300 feet long is said to have averaged $1\frac{1}{2}$ percent copper and 50 cents per ton in gold. A quartz porphyry dike about 200 feet wide, which strikes northwest for some 2000 feet, is said to assay from $2 to $8 per ton in gold. These claims have been idle in recent years except for assessment work.

Marath Mining Corporation included 120 acres of patented land in SE$\frac{1}{4}$ sec. 7, T. 46 N., R. 6 W., M. D., owned by Varil S. Nimes and wife, Box 25, Hornbrook. An andesite dike 35 feet wide, having numerous quartz stringers, strikes northward between black slate walls, and dips vertically. It is developed by a crosscut west, 150 feet long to the dike, a drift south 100 feet long in the center of the dike, and a drift north along the east wall for 60 feet. A 75-foot vertical raise connects with a second adit 35 feet long. Nimes and his wife milled the ore from these developments by crushing with a 4- by 5-inch jaw crusher, followed by an 18-inch by 4-foot-diameter ball mill, and concentrating with a Draper jig.

In 1946 the property was leased, with an option to purchase, to John M. and George Carras, a partnership, who formed the Mareth Mining Company with Carl Yates of Yreka as manager. Roads were built to the dike with a bulldozer, and a mill was built. Trucks were dumped over a grizzly with rails spaced at 8 inches, into a steel cylindrical ore bin 9 feet in diameter and 24 feet high. Material over $1\frac{1}{2}$-inches in size was crushed in a 9- by 16-inch jaw crusher driven by a "Jeep" motor operated on Butane fuel; it was then delivered to a second steel cylindrical fine-ore bin, 9 feet in diameter and 24 feet high, by a 14-inch belt conveyor 90 feet long inclined 10 percent above the horizontal. Material from the fine-ore bin was fed to a 3- by 4-foot Straub ball mill driven by 5 "V" belts from a "Jeep" engine. A 40-mesh screen-wheel classifier returned oversize to the ball mill and the fines to a Draper jig. Jig tailing was run over a 2- by 10-foot corduroy table. Concentrate was treated in an arrastre-type amalgamator. Mill heads were said to average from $6 to $7 per ton and tailing assayed 90 cents to $1.20 per ton. About 300 tons were milled between August 30 and November 15, 1946, when the property was shut down. The mill capacity was too small for this low-grade ore. Two men were employed at the mine and three men at the mill, on one shift. Mining equipment remaining at the property includes a Caterpillar bulldozer; a 10- by 10-inch Ingersoll-Rand compressor; an S-49 Ingersoll jackhammer with shell and column; a supply of 1-inch hexagonal drill steel and Timken bits; two mine cars; rails, picks, shovels, and hand tools sufficient to resume mining on a small scale.

Mattoon mine, in sec. 34, T. 45 N., R. 9 W., M. D., was operated by Amox Ginn of Fort Jones with a crew of four men in May 1937. Gravel was dug by a power shovel with a three-fourths-cubic-yard bucket, loaded onto trucks of 1½-cubic-yard capacity, and hauled to a washing plant consisting of a trommel, sluices, and belt tailing stacker. The plant was said to have had a capacity of 250 yards in an 8-hour shift. The property is idle. (Averill 31, p. 60; 35, p. 323.)

Mayland Mining Company is described under the White Bear Mine.

Middle Fork Mines. A. O. Witte of Redding has leased, with an option to purchase, two quartz claims owned by Everett Crouch, and four adjoining quartz claims owned by Lowell Hall on the Middle Fork of Humbug Creek in sec. 11, T. 45 N., R. 8 W., M. D. Quartz stringers and narrow veins occur in a soft medium-grained granodiorite near a contact with fine-grained hornblende diorite. The quartz stringers have been crushed and broken. They are commonly stained yellow and brown with limonite, and occasionly stained black with manganese. The Hall claims have been prospected by numerous shallow pits and short adits. On the Crouch claims, a caved adit is said to be 120 feet long with an 80-foot vertical raise to the surface on a vein 12 to 36 inches wide with granite walls. An old trestle from the adit and a small mill with a 3-by 4-foot ball mill are in a wrecked condition.

Witte has built a small mill on the Hall claims consisting of a 30-inch square hopper with a steel-rod grizzly spaced at 1 inch. Undersize drops through about 12 feet of 12-inch-diameter steel pipe to a 5- by 7-foot fine-ore bin 8 feet deep. The ore is fed by a disc feeder to a Huntington mill 5 feet in diameter and 30 inches deep, and ground through 35-mesh slotted screens. The crushed ore is run through a five-pan cascade-type amalgamator with 20-inch square pans fitted with 5- by 20-inch copper plates, and having one-eighth-inch holes for the pulp to drop through from pan to pan. The tailing is run through 20 feet of sluice boxes 10 inches wide and 2½ inches deep, lined with corduroy. Power is supplied by a De Soto automobile engine. One man is employed.

Midland Company, Inc., a partnership of Fred Hoyer and Elmer Dick of Sawyers Bar, commenced operating a dragline dredge on the North Fork of Salmon River 3 miles west of Sawyers Bar in November 1940. They had leases on 4 miles of land along the river. Equipment included a Lorain dragline with 55-foot boom, and a 1½-cubic-yard bucket powered by a Caterpillar D-13000 engine. The washing plant was floated on four 10- by 30- by 3½-foot wooden pontoons. The trommel was 4 by 30 feet and had 23 feet of three-eighths- to one-half-inch holes. The stacker belt was 28 inches wide and 45 feet long. The sluice boxes were 48 inches wide and there were three cross sluices and two downstream sluices on one side, and six cross sluices and two downstream sluices on the other side. They were fitted with expanded metal over cocoa matting. Power was furnished by an 85-horsepower Fairbanks-Morse diesel engine with a 1500-watt generator for electric lights. The gravel was 12 feet deep above a hard serpentine bedrock. There were many medium-size boulders. About 1600 cubic yards of gravel was dug in two shifts. Nine men were employed.

The dredge has been fitted with a single steel bucket about 6 feet wide with a 6- by 30-foot metal slide attached on the back end. It is designed to be lowered between two pontoons for digging, and then elevated by steel ropes through sheaves mounted on steel frame towers rising above the pontoons. The rock will slide into the hopper of the washing plant when the bucket is elevated. This design was never operated because the war closed gold-mining operations. It stands idle on the river about a mile below Sawyers Bar. A. C. Crawford is in charge.

Moccasin mine is owned by Larsen Brothers and Harms Brothers, Route 4, Box 2220, Sacramento, California. Dredging started in January 1940 on a strip of land half a mile wide and 2 miles long on the Klamath River near Horse Creek, in secs. 14 and 15, T. 46 N., R. 10 W., M. D. Equipment included a Bucyrus-Monighan Model-5W, Walker-type dragline with a 100-foot boom and a $4\frac{1}{2}$-cubic-yard bucket. Power was furnished by a 250-horsepower Fairbanks-Morse diesel engine. The Bodinson-built washing plant had eight steel pontoons making a barge 48 by 64 feet. The trommel is 6 feet in diameter and 47 feet long, with 30 feet of three-eighths- to three-fourths-inch holes. Water was supplied by a 14-inch United Iron Works centrifugal pump driven by a 100-horsepower General Electric motor, and a Sterling 4-inch centrifugal pump driven by a Wisconsin gasoline engine. The 42-inch stacker belt was 85 feet long. Power was furnished by a 300-horsepower Fairbanks-Morse diesel engine which drove a 200-kilavolt-amperes Fairbanks-Morse generator. There were 12 sluice boxes 29 inches wide feeding three downstream sluice boxes 29 inches wide on each side of the barge. They were fitted with Hungarian riffles and rubber mercury traps. The gravel was 25 to 45 feet deep above a soft schist bedrock. The operators were digging 6000 cubic yards in 24 hours in July 1941. Overburden was removed with a LeTourneau 12-cubic-yard carryall drawn by a D-8 Caterpillar tractor. A camp consisting of eight two-room cottages was built for employees about 3 miles above Horse Creek. This dredge was shut down June 25, 1946, and moved to Happy Camp in August, when it was renamed Scandia No. 2 dredge.

Mount Vernon Mines, Inc., comprises 70 acres of patented, and 40 acres of unpatented land in sec. 26, T. 45 N., R. 8 W., M. D. Kenneth K. Ash, Box 916, Yreka, is president and general manager. In October 1945, a horizontal diamond-drill hole was started in a S. 28° W. direction in the face of No. 6 adit. At 500 feet the hole turned downward 7 degrees and continued on that slope to bottom at 2084 feet. Between the depths of 39 feet 10 inches and 52 feet, the core was reported to assay $14 per ton in gold. The hole was run through greenstone, which showed pyrite and numerous thin seams of quartz in many cores. It was sampled and assayed at 5-foot intervals and is said to have cut quartz veins 32 inches wide assaying $4 per ton at 1150 feet, 16 inches wide assaying $30 per ton at 1200 feet, and 12 inches wide assaying $9 per ton at 1250 feet. Some gold was reported in all but a few assays from some 500 samples. At 900 feet the drill encountered a greenstone breccia from which water flowed at 80-pound pressure. A second hole on the Gold Road claim is reported to have cored 300 feet of greenstone.

Equipment included a Sullivan Machinery Company "Beauty" diamond drill driven by a Star automobile engine mounted on a steel frame, and a Gould New Pyramid pump driven by a Wisconsin air-cooled gasoline engine, Type A.K., size $2\frac{7}{8}$ by $2\frac{3}{4}$ inches. When it was decided to continue the hole beyond 1200 feet, a Knight and Stone diamond drill powered by a Model "A" Ford engine, and a Triplex pump driven by a Stratton gasoline engine, were substituted for the lighter equipment. Harold Johnson of Yreka was the drill operator on this job, and one assistant was employed. Studies made of the diamond-drill core suggest that there may be wide zones in the greenstones that could provide ore for a low-grade cyanide operation. (Brown 16, p. 837; Laizure 21, p. 534; Tucker 23, p. 11; Logan 25, p. 452; Averill 31, p. 45; 35, pp. 299-300, 323.)

Norcal Mining Company owned a group of claims about 5 miles south of Sawyers Bar in sec. 16, T. 39 N., R. 11 W., M. D. The group included the Ida May, Francis Ball, and Lucky Strike claims, which were sold to Jack Usher of Sawyers Bar, and are now part of the Security group. The Norcal Company has not operated since 1938. (Averill 35, pp. 261, 301, 324.)

Okoro Mines, Inc., Carl Weinhager Jr., St. Paul, Minnesota, president, operated a dragline dredge on the Scott River near Callahan on land owned by R. V. Hayden of Callahan. At first the operation employed a Marion dragline with a 2-cubic-yard bucket and a "dry land" washing plant built by the Bodinson Company on a steel chassis with Caterpillar treads $12\frac{1}{2}$ inches wide and 30 feet long. The trommel was 54 inches in diameter, 28 feet long, with 18 feet of three-fourths- to seven-sixteenths- and five-sixteenths-inch holes. Jigs were used in place of sluice boxes. Recovery was said to have been satisfactory, but the plant was discarded in June 1940 because the gravel was too deep for the equipment. Costs were up to 25 cents per yard and the gravel was only yielding 20 cents per yard. The washing plant was remodeled and a wooden hull 34 by 52 feet and 4 feet deep was built of 6-inch plank with asphalt joints, strengthened with wooden trusses and steel cables and tie rods at 4-foot intervals. The trommel was 54 inches in diameter and 28 feet long, with 18 feet of three-fourths- to five-sixteenths-inch holes. The stacker belt was 30 inches wide and 90 feet long, to take care of the expected depth of the gravel. A Dayton-Dowd impeller pump supplied 2500 gallons of water per minute. Steel sluices with Hungarian riffles were used in place of the jigs. This equipment was all electrically operated with power purchased from the California-Oregon Power Company. The plant had a capacity of 2500 yards per day to a maximum depth of 35 feet. The bedrock was hard. Test holes indicated that an average of 50 cents per yard could be mined, but in January 1942 only 103 ounces of gold and 10 ounces of silver were recovered from 60,000 yards. The operation was shut down. Fourteen men were employed under Lynn Rood, manager.

Oom Paul mine has one claim in sec. 12, T. 43 N., R. 10 W., M. D., and is owned by Lawrence A. Whipple of Greenview. It is leased with an option to purchase by Joe Meaders and Jerry Carlson. A quartz vein 4 to 20 inches wide strikes N. 35° W. and dips 50° N. The quartz is broken and stained brown, red, and black, and includes some "sugar" quartz and some with small vug holes. Both walls are andesite that is cracked and seamed. A quartz diorite dike 4 feet wide parallels the vein a short distance away along the hanging wall. An adit has been driven on the vein for 50 feet. Meaders and Carlson are driving the adit ahead in the hope of developing sufficient ore to justify a small milling plant.

Oro Grande Mining Company (McKeen mine) owns 480 acres of patented land in sec. 36, T. 40 N., R. 9 W., M. D. It was under lease to Oils Incorporated in 1939. Six mineral-separation cells were added to the mill circuit, but the recovery was said to have been poor and the lease was abandoned in June 1940 after about 6 months of operation. Mill heads were said to have averaged $9.65 per ton. Hugh McKinney of Callahan, president of the company, claims that there is a recorded production of $250,000 from the property and that 25,000 tons of ore averaging $12 per ton is blocked out. This property is described in detail by Averill (31, p. 48). (Crawford 96, p. 419; Hamilton 22, p. 17; Brown 16, p. 838; Laizure 21, p. 534; Logan 25, pp. 453-454; Averill 35, pp. 302, 325.)

Quartz Hill mine includes about 75 acres of patented land on the Scott River at Scott Bar in sec. 16, T. 45 N., R. 10 W., M.D., owned by George C., Fannie E., and Emma L. Noonan of Scott Bar. Many rich pockets of gold have been recovered at this mine since it was first discovered in 1852. The gold occurs in quartz stringers and lenses in a gray to black micaceous schist. It is associated with fine-grained pyrite, and sometimes with galena. The mine was first worked by hydraulic methods and later by blasting the rock loose from the face and washing it through sluice boxes. Some of the quartz lenses have been mined by drifts and shafts, and the quartz milled in a 10-stamp mill. In 1941-42 George Noonan and George Milne had two men employed mining a quartz lens 4½ feet wide from an adit driven N. 83° E. for about 50 feet. They erected a timber headframe above a 75-foot incline shaft and mined a quartz vein from an old drift driven 180 feet east at the bottom of the shaft. A few pockets were mined in this work and the gold was recovered by grinding to 50-mesh in an Ellis mill and amalgamating on a copper plate 14 inches wide and 7 feet long.

The property was idle during the war, but in May 1947 Harry M. Thompson had a lease with an option to purchase and had 8 men employed prospecting the mine. Equipment included a Byers 83 power shovel and an Allis-Chalmers No. 10 bulldozer. The old 10-stamp mill was being put in shape to operate. Thompson says that the silver and gold telluride, petzite, is present in the ore. (Dunn 93, p. 447; Crawford 94, p. 290; 96, p. 421; Brown 16, p. 824; Averill 31, p. 49; 34, p. 307; 35, pp. 303, 325.)

Rainbow mine (Victory Gold Mines) includes four patented quartz claims, nineteen unpatented quartz claims, and four placer claims in secs. 16, 17, and 20, T. 40 N., R. 10 W., M.D. They were purchased in 1935 from the Victory Mines Company by the Rainbow Gold Mining Company, a Washington corporation controlled by William Winter and Son of Etna, California. Three men were employed prospecting quartz stringers in black schist in 1941. No production has been made for more than 10 years. (Logan 25, p. 459; Averill 35, pp. 311, 328.)

Roxbury Placer owns the Michigan Bar, Thomas, Junction Bar, and Johnson associated placer claims, which include 640 acres of patented land in secs. 6, 7, and 8, T. 45 N., R. 10 W., M.D. T. S. Rodgers of Spokane, Washington, leased this property and employed two men from September 1940 to June 1941 driving a 400-foot adit. He found that some of the old channel already had been drifted. Clarence Paulson of Spokane, and Edward F. Weber of Yreka prospected the property for possible dredging, but no operation resulted. The property was purchased from Henry L. Day of Wallace, Idaho, by James J. and Charles H. Brown of Scott Bar on August 20, 1946. (Logan 25, p. 484; Averill 35, pp. 257, 326.)

Sacchi-Spellenberg Mines. P. D. Sacchi, E. L. Spellenberg, and F. Kubli of Arcata operated a Judson Pacific dragline dredge with a 1½-cubic-yard bucket on the Salmon River near Forks of Salmon in 1939-40. The equipment was sold to Salmon River Dredging Company.

Salmon River Gold Dredging Company. George G. Titzell, 310 Kearney, Street, San Francisco, and J. P. Wood, Forks of Salmon, general partners, operated a dragline dredge on the Salmon River near Forks of Salmon and Sawyers Bar, and on the Klamath River near Happy Camp in 1941. Equipment was purchased from the Northern Dredging Company and included a Lima 1201 dragline with an 80-foot boom, a 2¾-cubic-yard Esco bucket, and a 250-horsepower Cummins diesel engine. The Bodinson washing plant was built of five steel pontoons making a hull 36 by 44 feet. The trommel was 54 inches in diameter and 28 feet long with an 18-foot length of screen. The stacker was 30 inches wide by 60 feet long. Water was supplied by a 12-inch United Iron Works centrifugal pump. There were nine 30-inch cross sluices, and three 30-inch downstream sluices on each side fitted with metal Hungarian riffles. Power was furnished by a Caterpillar D-13000 engine. F. A. Warren, Forks of Salmon, was dredgemaster.

Salmon River Mines Company (Trail Creek mine), E. C. Latcham, president and general manager, V. W. Peterson, secretary, Callahan, own seven claims in sec. 12, T. 39 N., R. 10 W., M.D. A quartz-stringer zone 5 feet wide is said to assay $12 in gold in the face of an adit 950 feet long. A 50-ton Marcy ball mill, 6 flotation cells, and other equipment for a small mill are said to have been purchased, but installation was delayed because of the war. (Averill 35, p. 307.)

Schroeder mine includes five patented and eight unpatented claims in sec. 17, T. 45 N., R. 8 W., M.D. Owner is Fidelity Metals Corporation, 2989 21st Avenue, San Francisco; agent is Major H. A. White, Yreka. In 1941 a partnership composed of Major White, George C. Phares, and two others had a lease and option, and the property was operated for a short time. The "1600" tunnel was reopened, and a winze was sunk to a depth of 96 feet on a vein 6 to 10 inches wide, striking N. 85° W. and dipping 74° S. Drifts were run 70 feet east and 40 feet west at the bottom of the winze. The vein was said to be 10 inches wide and to assay $40 per ton in the face of the east adit. The west drift was in waste because of a fault.

Equipment included a 3-drill capacity Ingersoll-Rand compressor, a Sullivan single-drum air hoist, and an air lift pump. The mill included a 6- by 8-inch Blake jaw crusher, a Straub ball mill grinding to 50-mesh, two 3- by 3½-foot amalgamating plates, and a Universal Overstrom table. Power was obtained by a Wisconsin 20-horsepower gasoline engine. The gold was said to be 85 percent free. The property has not been reopened since 1942. (Crawford 94, p. 291; 96, p. 424; Logan 25, p. 457; Averill 31, p. 53; 35, pp. 307, 326.)

Scandia No. 1 dredge, owned by Larsen Brothers and Harms Brothers, Route 4, Box 2220, Sacramento, was operating on Horse Creek in sec. 7, T. 46 N., R. 10 W., M.D., in December 1946. They purchased the mineral rights on a strip of land a quarter of a mile wide for a length of 4 miles along Horse Creek from its junction with the Klamath River, and started dredging in section 15 in December 1938. It was stipulated that the soil would be stripped from meadowland, the tailings leveled, and the soil restored. This has been done. Equipment included a Marion 40-A dragline with a 60-foot boom using a 3-cubic-yard bucket. Power was furnished by a Cummins 250-horsepower diesel engine. The Bodinson washing plant had 8 steel pontoons making a hull 48 by 56 feet. The trommel was 60 inches in diameter, 42 feet long with 30 feet of five-sixteenths- to three-fourths-inch holes. Stacker belt was 36 inches wide and 60 feet long, and was operated by a 15-horsepower General Electric motor. Water was pumped by a United Iron Works 10-inch centrifugal pump, and a Rex speed prime 4-inch centrifugal pump. Power was furnished by a Caterpillar D-17000 engine. Electric lights were provided by a 1500-watt Koehler light plant. There were 12 cross sluice boxes 30 inches wide, and 2 downstream sluice boxes 30 inches wide on each side, fitted with Hungarian riffles.

The gravel was 15 to 18 feet deep above a soft black schist, and the operators were digging about 3500 yards in three shifts in December 1946. Cinnabar was found in the sands but was not saved. The top soil was about 2 feet deep in section 7, and a 200-yard width was stripped with a LeTourneau 12-cubic-yard carryall pulled by a D-8 Caterpillar tractor. The tailing from the dredge was leveled with a D-8 Caterpillar bulldozer and the soil replaced evenly for planting new crops. Eleven men were employed under R. I. Barritt, dredgemaster.

Scandia No. 2 (Moccasin) dredge, owned by Larsen Brothers and Harms Brothers, Route 4, Box 2220, Sacramento, was moved from the Klamath River near Horse Creek to claims in sec. 15, T. 16 N., R. 7 E., H., owned by Mrs. M. McCulloch of Medford, Oregon, and Joe Most of Seattle, Washington. Two extra pontoons 3 by 20 by 4 feet were added to each side of the hull to give it greater stability. Digging started on November 10, 1946. The gravel was 25 feet deep above a medium-hard black slate bedrock. Fifteen men were employed under Ray C. Henrici, dredgemaster.

Scott Bar Mines, Inc., includes 71.7 acres of patented land in secs. 16 and 21, T. 45 N., R. 10 W., M.D., owned by George A. Milne, Fort Jones. It adjoins the Quartz Hill mine on the east and is in the same formation of black micaceous schist with many stringers and lenses of white quartz. A quartz vein is developed by a 6- by 10-foot incline shaft 165 feet deep on a 40° slope in a N. 17° E. direction. Drifts were run on the vein at 100-, 155- and 165-foot depths. A fault at the bottom of the shaft strikes S. 15° E. and dips 40° south. A crosscut south is being driven to find the vein beneath the fault. The gold occurs in pockets in the white quartz and is associated with pyrite and galena. Several rich pockets have been mined from this property, which has a recorded production of over $41,000 from development work or an average of $10.93 per ton of rock excavated. Equipment includes a single-drum hoist driven by a Dodge engine, an Ingersoll-Rand 240-cubic-foot compressor, two Ingersoll-Rand jackhammer drills with shells and mountings, drill steel and accessory tools necessary to develop a small mine. A Sullivan core drill, Class H.S.15 has been purchased together with 300 feet of rods, three Model-7100A-C bevel bits, a Gardner-Denver 3- by 2- by 3-inch duplex pump, and an Ingersoll-Rand 315-cubic-foot portable air compressor. A diamond core-drilling development is planned. There is a small mill on the property which includes a jaw crusher, Ellis ball mill Type B1 with 40-mesh slotted screens, and a

$2\frac{1}{2}$- by 3-foot amalgamation plate. The jaw crusher is driven by a 3-horse-power Fuller Johnson gasoline engine, and the Ellis mill by a 3-horsepower John Deere gasoline engine. From three to six men are employed on development.

Security mine includes 7 unpatented claims in sec. 15, T. 39 N., R. 11 W., M.D., owned by John W. Usher of Sawyers Bar. An adit on the Soon Parted claim cut a 4-foot quartz vein striking northeast and dipping flatly southeast. The Soon Parted and Sandwich claims are leased to Melvin L. Usher and Leslie E. Dunbar, who plan to develop the vein and to install a 5-stamp mill on the property.

Siskiyou County mine includes 5 claims in sec. 31, T. 18 N., R. 7 E., H., owned by the James L. Wortham estate, Los Angeles, California. In November 1946 Leonard Crumpton of Happy Camp had a 5-year lease on this property and was repairing the ditch and pipe line from Mill Creek and preparing to operate. The bank is about 60 feet high with about 20 feet of gravel above a slate bedrock. There are many boulders that will have to be blasted or moved with a derrick. (Averill 35, p. 308.)

Smith and Myers mine. A small hydraulic mine was operated by Smith and Myers in 1941. It is located in Whites Gulch in sec. 26, T. 40 N., R. 11 W., M.D., about 3 miles east of Sawyers Bar. Water was brought from Whites Gulch through about a mile of ditch and flume and delivered to two No. 2 giants with 4-inch nozzles under 200-foot head. The gravel was washed through sluice boxes 3 feet wide, fitted with block riffles.

Starveout placer includes 3 claims on Arastra Creek in sec. 24, T. 48 N., R. 8 W., M.D., owned by R. A. Myers and R. A. Smith. Quartz stringers weathered from granodiorite are washed into a 12- by 12-inch sluice box 12 feet long fitted with Hungarian riffles. Water is obtained from a spring through about 100 feet of 12- by 12-inch flume, and is collected in a sump behind an earth-filled dam 9 feet high and 10 feet wide. Water for sluicing is pumped by a Jacuzzi Brothers $2\frac{1}{2}$-inch centrifugal pump driven by a V belt from a Dodge automobile engine, and is discharged through 300 feet of fire hose having a seven-eighths inch nozzle. The loose weathered material that can be sluiced is 8 to 10 inches deep and yields some coarse gold.

Stenshaw (Klamath Gold Mining Corporation), Charles P. Franchot, president, Room 1636, 60 East 42nd Street, New York, N. Y., operated a hydraulic mine on the Klamath River about 9 miles above Somes Bar in secs. 28, 29, and 32, T. 13 N., R. 6 E., H., in 1937. Water was obtained under 250-foot head from Sandy Bar Creek through 1200 feet of flume and 2000 feet of 18- and 14-inch pipe, and from Stenshaw Creek under a 125-foot head by 500 feet of flume and 1200 feet of 18-, 16-, and 14-inch pipe. The gravel was about 25 feet deep above a soft slate bedrock and included many boulders that had to be blasted and lifted with a derrick. A No. 3 giant with $4\frac{1}{2}$-inch nozzle, and a No. 4 giant with a 5-inch nozzle, were used in the pit. There were 500 feet of sluice boxes, 120 feet of which were fitted with angle iron and iron-shod wooden riffles. A Linco Engineering Company gold-saving machine was used in testing gravel and in cleaning up. It consisted of a small trommel and a centrifugal bowl, driven by a $3\frac{1}{2}$-horsepower gasoline engine. The gravel was said to have averaged 25 cents per cubic yard. Eight men were employed in April 1937. There has been no recent operation. (Irelan 88, p. 604; Crawford 95, p. 428; Logan 25, p. 487; Averill 35, p. 327.)

Sunnyslope (Mullen) mine includes 5 claims in sec. 2, T. 40 N., R. 9 W., M.D., owned by J. A. Richter of Callahan. A quartz vein 2 to 7 feet wide strikes S. 25° W., and dips steeply east. It has been crushed and broken and is stained yellow and brown from the oxidation of included pyrite. The walls are a fine-grained dark-gray rock, probably andesite. The Carry adit was driven N. 10° W. 70 feet to the vein, and then S. 25° W. for 50 feet on the vein, which was 5 feet wide at the face. About 8 tons of ore from this vein was ground to 40-mesh in a 2- by 5-foot ball mill driven by an International 5-horsepower gasoline engine. It is said to have yielded $70 in gold by amalgamation. No assays have been made to determine gold in the sulphides. The vein has been traced for over 500 feet on the surface by shallow shafts and trenches. Richter has been working alone on the property. (Averill 31, p. 47; 35, p. 324.)

Swede (Hickey) placer is owned by John Teuhert and leased to C. F. Thomain and Dan Sagaser of Sawyers Bar. It is in sec. 27, T. 40 N., R. 12 W., M.D., about 7 miles west of Sawyers Bar. Water is obtained from Alder Gulch through a ditch a mile long, and delivered through 120 feet of 11-inch pipe at a 108-foot head to a No. 2 giant with a 4-inch nozzle. There are 24 feet of sluice boxes 18 inches wide fitted with Hungarian riffles. The gravel bank is 30 feet high above a granite and serpentine bedrock. Boulders are plentiful. Operations were just starting when the property was visited March 21, 1947. (Crawford 94, p. 284.)

Trail Creek mine, see Salmon River Mines Company.

Vest Mining Company is a partnership composed of Frank Vest and Alfred Peeler of Seattle, Washington. They were operating a hydraulic mine in sec. 33, T. 40 N., R. 12 W., M.D., in March 1947. Water was obtained from Jones Creek through half a mile of ditch and 1500 feet of 36- to 15-inch steel pipeline. It was delivered under 120 feet of head to a giant fitted with a 2½-inch nozzle. A bank of angular gravel about 20 feet high was washed down to reach an old channel, a part of which was worked as a drift mine about 8 years ago by a miner named Neenach. The bedrock is decomposed granite. About 300 feet of 24- by 24-inch sluice boxes fitted with block riffles has been built. A derrick to handle boulders is operated by a double-drum hoist connected to a 36-inch Pelton water wheel. Four men were employed under Henry Seibert, foreman.

War Horse group of 13 claims in sec. 9, T. 45 N., R. 8 W., M.D., is owned by W. H. Price of Yreka. It is developed by an adit whose portal is about 300 feet west of and 60 feet higher than the No. 5 adit of the Eliza mine. The adit was driven S. 77° W. for 290 feet to a 12-inch quartz vein striking north and dipping 54° E. There are about 3 inches of black gouge on both walls of the vein which was said to assay $42.90 per ton. The quartz was said to assay $4 per ton in gold. The old Boyle mine is over the hill about half a mile to the west. The property is idle except for assessment work.

Webber Dredge (von der Hellen and Webber). Edward F. Webber, Box 217, Yreka, operated a dragline dredge on Humbug Creek about 2 miles south of the Klamath River in sec. 29, T. 46 N., R. 7 W., M.D. The dredge started at the mouth of Clear Creek in October 1939 as the von der Hellen and Webber dredge and reworked tailing from earlier placer-mining operations. In 1941 the dredge was purchased and operated by E. F. Webber. Equipment included a Lima dragline with a 60-foot boom and a 2-yard Esco bucket. It was powered by a Caterpillar D-17000 engine. The Judson Pacific washing plant was built of 5 steel pontoons making a hull 34 by 42 feet. The trommel was 60 inches in diameter and 30 feet long with 20 feet of three-eighths- to five-eighths-inch slots. Power was furnished by a Caterpillar D-13000 engine. The stacker belt was 30 inches wide and 60 feet long between pulleys. There were 8 cross sluices 31 inches wide and 8 to 14 feet long discharging into 3 downstream sluices, 31 inches wide and 36 feet long, on each side. They were fitted with Hungarian riffles and mercury traps. In September 1941 the operators were digging about 100 tons per hour. The gravel was about 8 feet deep above a rough, hard bedrock, probably slate. There were many boulders. This equipment was moved to the Klamath River near McKinney Creek in sec. 9, T. 46 N., R. 9 W., M.D., on land owned by F. A. Jackson. It was shut down in September 1942 because of shortages of labor and supplies caused by the war. Some of the equipment was sent to war industries. Operations had not been resumed in March 1947.

West Branch Dredging Company is a partnership composed of Leslie G. Allen, G. B. Sutton, Donald Miller, Willard Landrum, and John Glassner of Fort Jones, California. The Beaver Dredging Company equipment was purchased in May 1942. The company owns 80 acres along Indian Creek in sec. 35, T. 45 N., R. 9 W., M.D. The gravel is from 6 to 12 feet deep above a slate and schist bedrock and is all old placer tailing. The equipment is the same as described under the Beaver Dredging Company except that the Model 1201 Lima Dragline has been replaced by a Model 6 Northwest dragline with a 50-foot boom, a 1½-cubic-yard bucket, and a Twin City gasoline engine. The equipment has been idle since June 1946.

White Bear mine (Mayland Mining Company) includes a group of 10 unpatented claims about 7 miles south of Sawyers Bar in sec. 18, 19, T. 39 N., R. 11 W., M.D. It is owned by the Mayland Mining Company, Harry J. Mills, managing director, and W. A. Harvey, mining engineer, Sawyers Bar. The property has been idle since the mill burned down about 10 years ago. The mine maps and assays indicate that quite a large tonnage of ore averaging $5 per ton in gold has been developed by drifts and raises from four adits. The last production was recorded in 1936. Manganese minerals outcropping on this property are described under "Mayland Mining Company," listed with manganese deposits. (Brown 16, p. 842; Averill 35, p. 311.)

White placer mine consists of two claims in sec. 12, T. 45 N., R. 8 W., M.D., owned by F. O. Jensen, Box 12, Yreka. Jensen and his son have been ground-sluicing these claims since 1938. Water for a No. 2 giant is obtained from Keeler Creek under about 100 feet of head. The gravel is sluiced through 120 feet of 24-by 16-inch boxes, the first 20 feet fitted with Hungarian riffles, the remaining 100 feet with pole riffles. The mine is worked 4 to 5 months each year while water is available.

Yreka Gold Dredging Company, 351 California Street, San Francisco, moved from Yreka Creek, just north of Yreka, and started operating on the Klamath River at Seiad in sec. 13, T. 46 N., R., 12 W., M.D., September 16, 1941. A detailed description of this bucket-line dredge is given by Averill (38, p. 123; 46, p. 300). A separate winch driven by a 40-horsepower General Electric motor was installed for the digging ladder. The ladder was lengthened 10 feet and the stacker belt 15 feet. At the Seiad location they were digging 20 feet of gravel and 2 feet of soft granite bedrock. Prospecting was done with a Keystone portable drill, and 6-inch holes were drilled at 100-foot intervals. Equipment includes an R.D.6 Caterpillar tractor, a D-6 Bulldozer, a 5-cubic-yard

LeTourneau carryall. A 1¾-cubic-yard Northwest dragline is used for digging canals and building levees. Twenty men are employed on three 8-hour shifts under Eric S. Peterson, dredgemaster. The Yreka Gold Dredging Company is consolidated with Arroyo Secco Gold Dredging Company of Ione, California, who own 277 acres in secs. 12, 13, and 14, T. 46 N., R. 12 W., M.D. (Averill 38, p. 123; 46, pp. 300-303.)

Yuba Consolidated Gold Fields (Siskiyou Unit), 351 California Street, San Francisco, California, owns a strip of land about 4 miles long and 1400 to 2700 feet wide along the Scott River in secs. 6 and 7, T. 40 N., R. 8 W.; sec. 1, T. 40 N., R. 9 W.; sec. 31, T. 41 N., R. 8 W.; and secs. 25 and 36, T. 41 N., R. 9 W., M.D.

The Yuba No. 116 bucket-line dredge was built on sec. 7, T. 40 N., R. 8 W., in 1936. It has a steel hull 122 feet 8 inches by 56 feet, and 10 feet deep. The digging ladder is 93 feet long with 70 buckets, capacity 9 cubic feet each, and they are pulled at the rate of 22 to 24 buckets per minute by a 350-horsepower Westinghouse motor. The trommel is 8 feet in diameter and 48 feet long, with 34 feet of three-eighths- to five-eighths-inch holes, and is rotated at 7 revolutions per minute by a 75-horsepower Westinghouse motor. The stacker belt is 36 inches wide and 136 feet long between pulleys and is operated by a 50-horsepower motor. A Byron-Jackson high-pressure 12-inch centrifugal pump is operated by a 100-horsepower motor, and a 12-inch centrifugal low-pressure pump is operated by a 50-horsepower motor. On each side of the trommel the cross sluice boxes are double banked with four 32-inch sluices above eleven 32-inch cross sluices discharging into nine 32-inch downstream sluices fitted with steel-shod wooden riffles. The swing winch is operated by a 50-horsepower electric motor. Water pumped by a 6-inch Byron-Jackson centrifugal pump driven by a 40-horsepower motor was used to wash the gravel in the hopper; a 4-inch Byron-Jackson centrifugal pump was used in the clean-up and for fire protection.

In June 1941, a Yuba bucket idler was installed, which made it possible to dig an additional 5 feet in depth to a maximum of 40 feet. The gravel in sec. 1, T. 40 N., R. 9 W. was only 12 feet deep above a hard serpentine bedrock, but test holes have shown 36 to 52 feet of gravel ahead. The boat was operated 24 hours per day with 11 men on the dredge crew, one caterpiller bulldozer operator, two shoremen, one retortman, one electrician, one carpenter, one machinist, two shopmen, one truckdriver, and one field clerk, a total of 22 men, under W. B. Lewis, dredgemaster. The dredge was shut down April 15, 1946, and it was planned to add three rollers and an additional 21 feet in length to the digging ladder. Four additional pontoons had been added to the hull and it was planned to add two more. There will be 75 buckets on the line when the remodeling is completed. About 3 years operation remains at this location. (Averill 38, p. 126.)

Zarina mine includes nine unpatented claims in sec. 27, T. 41 N., R. 10 W., M.D., owned by John J. Stanning of Etna, California. A quartz vein 2 feet wide with schist walls was developed by two adits and drifts and stopes. The property has been idle for many years and the adits are caved at the portals. The mine buildings, with the exception of one log cabin, are all wrecked. There is no mine equipment at the property. (Brown 16, pp. 822, 842; Averill 35, p. 329.)

Graphite

Black Jack (Crystal, Elk Lake) group of three claims and a mill site in sec. 12. T. 47 N., R. 12 W., M. D., were located by Elwood R. and William B. Stewart, Mrs. Cora Maddron, and W. H. Gassoway, in 1941. They are reached by about a mile of rough trail from the Forest Service road at the Cook and Green Pass. Graphite occurs finely disseminated in sandstone and in cracks and narrow seams near a contact with andesite. Very little prospecting has been done on these claims and no attempt has been made to determine the grade of ore that might be produced.

Limestone

Many large deposits of limestone and marble outcrop in Siskiyou County, and those located favorably in regard to roads and railroad transportation have been mined from time to time. The deposits outcropping about 3 miles west of the railroad at Gazelle are mined, processed, and sold as agricultural limestone, "carbide rock", road metal, and for use in sugar refining. They are the closest source of agricultural limestone for areas in Oregon with soils deficient in that necessary mineral.

Electro Lime and Chemical Corporation, C. J. Montag, president, Dr. L. Underdahl, vice-president, P. M. Sherlund, treasurer, and G. R. Bethel, secretary, have offices at 536 Southeast Sixth Avenue, Portland, Oregon. The limestone is mined from a deposit in secs. 4, 5, and 8, T. 42 N., R. 6 W., M.D., owned by Sisto Mazzuchi of Gazelle. It is drilled by two men using jackhammers on wagon-drill mountings. Holes are spaced at 5-foot intervals, drilled 20 feet vertically, loaded with 40-percent dynamite, and blasted. The broken limestone is loaded onto dump trucks with a 1-cubic-yard Lorain shovel and hauled 3 miles to the crushing and screening plant at Gazelle. There it is dumped into a 20-ton-capacity wooden bin from a ramp and fed into a 24- by 36-inch jaw crusher by a 30-inch Lipman feeder. The jaw crusher discharges minus 3-inch material onto a 24-inch conveyor belt 70 feet long which delivers it to a 3- by 10-foot Pioneer double-deck vibrating screen driven by a $7\frac{1}{2}$-horsepower motor. Material over $1\frac{1}{2}$-inches and under $\frac{1}{2}$-inch is delivered to a 3XC-type Grundler hammer mill driven by a 220-horsepower diesel engine. The $1\frac{1}{2}$- to $\frac{1}{2}$-inch size goes to a bin for sale as "carbide rock". The hammer-mill product is raised 28 feet with a bucket elevator to a 4- by 12-foot, 3-deck Seco vibrating screen fitted with 8-mesh screens. The oversize is stockpiled. The undersize is classed as agricultural limestone and is weighed by an "OK" weighing machine into paper bags holding 100 pounds each, or is loaded in bulk on cars or trucks for shipment. Material sold for agricultural limestone is specified as 100 percent minus 8-mesh, 50 percent minus 50-mesh, and 35 percent minus 100-mesh. It has a minimum of 95 percent $CaCO_3$ and a maximum of 1 percent $MgCO_3$. Material from half an inch to $1\frac{1}{2}$ inches in size is classed as "carbide rock" and is used in the manufacture of calcium carbide.

Four men were employed at the quarry and seven men at the mill under George E. Bethel, superintendent, in May 1947. Production was at the rate of 150 tons per 8-hour day.

Mt. Shasta limestone deposit is located about 4 miles west of Gazelle in sec. 12, T. 42 N., R. 7 W., M.D. It is on patented land owned by E. M. Greenwood. It was leased and operated by M. C. Lininger and Sons, Medford, Oregon, in 1945. The limestone was broken in benches by drilling vertical holes about 20 feet deep spaced 5 feet apart, and blasting with 40-percent dynamite. The broken limestone was loaded into dump trucks with a three-fourths-cubic-yard Northwest power shovel. It was crushed in a 24- by 36-inch Telesmith jaw crusher and screened with a Symons vibrating screen having 2-inch and 6-inch screens. About 1200 tons of hard blue limestone between 2 and 6 inches in size was shipped each week on a 25,000-ton contract. It was used by a sugar refinery. Material under 2 inches in size was stockpiled. (Averill 35, pp. 331, 332.)

Lead

Balfrey (Siskiyou Lead) mine. Eight hundred acres of patented land in secs. 28 and 29, T. 41 N., R. 7 W., M.D., are owned by M. H. Balfrey of Etna, California. Small amounts of galena and fine-grained sphalerite, and rarely chalcopyrite, occur in shear zones in andesite. The sulphide minerals are accompanied in some places by calcite and barite. The old shafts and adits on this property are caved and inaccessible. Although showings of galena have been prospected by shallow pits in many places over these claims, the mineralization was not sufficient to encourage the operators to do much development work. All machinery and equipment have been removed from this property and it has been idle since 1929. (Averill 35, pp. 274, 314.)

Manganese

Manganese deposits occur in the western part of Siskiyou County, and prospects have been examined in the Fort Jones, Oro Fino, Happy Camp, Seiad Valley, and Sawyers Bar districts. Although some of the outcrops are quite extensive, the grade of the ore, and especially the high silica content, would not meet the minimum Metals Reserve Company specifications, and little ore was mined. Thirty-one manganese deposits in Siskiyou County were listed by Trask (43, pp. 183-185, map), a few of which are described here.

Colgrove Manganese (Fort Jones). W. J. Colgrove and Max Erwin of Fort Jones had three men employed mining and sorting manganese ore from an outcrop on patented land in sec. 2, T. 43 N., R. 9 W., M.D., leased from Frank Jordan of Fort Jones. The outcrop was about 12 feet wide between andesite walls. Pyrolusite was so intimately mixed with white quartz and brown limonite that sorting to meet the Metal Reserve Company specifications of May 1942 could not be done.

Fort Jones Manganese, see Colgrove manganese.

Gray Ledge mine is located on Music Creek about 2 miles east of Finley Camp in sec. 21, T. 40 N., R. 10 W., M.D. It was operated by E. A. von Gerlitz of Sawyers Bar, and W. B. Stewart of Fort Jones in 1943-44. They shipped 231 tons of manganese ore to the Metals Reserve Company stockpile at Yreka, which averaged 40 percent manganese and 15 percent silica. The chief minerals were rhodochrosite and hausmannite.

Jim Allen mine. One claim in sec. 8, T. 44 N., R. 8 W., M.D., is owned by John F. Lewis and Robert Reynolds of Fort Jones. In June 1942 it was under lease to Max Erwin and Ronald Knudsen of Yreka. A 23-foot width of black manganese streaked with spongy quartz and brown limonite was exposed in three bulldozer cuts. It was too high in silica to meet the Metals Reserve Company specifications and no production was recorded.

Mayland Mining Company (White Bear mine) holds 10 unpatented claims in secs. 18 and 19, T. 39 N., R. 11 W., M.D., about 7 miles south of Sawyers Bar. Bands of black manganese and white quartz with some pink rhodonite and rhodochrosite outcrop for a width of about 150 feet below the Sawyers Bar-Cecilville road. The manganese ore was too low in grade and too high in silica to meet the Metals Reserve Company specifications. (Trask 43, p. 184.)

Mineral Water

Shasta Water Company, J. J. Nagy, president, Sixth and Brannan Streets, San Francisco, California, owns Shasta Springs, located about 2 miles north of Dunsmuir in sec. 7, T. 39 N., R. 3 W., M. D. The natural carbonated water issuing from the spring is pumped into three 3500-gallon-capacity glass-lined steel tanks. It is allowed to settle for 3 days and is then decanted and pumped into railroad tank cars lined with block tin, and shipped to distributing plants in San Francisco, Seattle, Los Angeles, Portland, and Sacramento. The water is filtered through rock before bottling and is recharged with carbon dioxide. Herman Utah is superintendent at the springs.

The cabins and hotel accommodations available at Shasta Springs Resort are operated by the Thompson Hotel Company, Harry Price, manager. The springs of Siskiyou County are described in the following reports and bulletins: Crawford 96, p. 520; Watts 93, pp. 449-452; and G. A. Waring 15.

Stewart Mineral Springs in sec. 11, T. 41 N., R. 6 W., M. D., is owned and operated by Mrs. Kathryn Lloyd, Box 507, Edgewood, California. A cold-water spring said to contain medicinal minerals has been developed for drinking and bathing. There are 14 guest cabins with tub baths and a community kitchen and dining room. The water is heated for the baths.

Analysis of Stewart Springs water	P.P.M.
Total solids	3470.00
Volatile and organic matter	750.00
Alkalinity as $CaCO_3$	647.50
Silica	25.20
Iron and aluminum oxides	2.30
CaO	3.10
MgP_2O_7	Trace
SO_3	207.67
Chlorine	1014.28

Table Rock Spring, in sec. 20, T. 45 N., R. 4 W., M.D., is owned by the Sidney F. Terwilliger estate. No commercial production has been made from this spring since 1945. The water was formerly bottled as a carbonated natural mineral water by the Yreka Coca Cola Bottling Works, Fred J. Meamber, proprietor, 412 South Main Street, Yreka.

Analysis of Table Rock Spring water	P.P.M.
Silica	452
Iron and aluminum oxides	2.30
Aluminum oxide	21
Magnesium bicarbonate	128.8
Calcium bicarbonate	556.6
Sodium bicarbonate	3010.7
Sodium sulphate	4.3
Sodium chloride	797.1
Total solids	4545.1

Molybdenite

Molybdenite was present in the ore mined at the Yellow Butte mine mentioned above under the heading *Copper*.

Ornamental and Gem Stones

Californite ("California jade") is a very compact, massive green vesuvianite, which takes a high polish and resembles jade. It occurs as streaks and nodules in serpentine. The deposit on the *Chan jade claim* on the South Fork of Indian Creek about $10\frac{1}{2}$ miles north of Happy Camp, is owned by J. L. Kraft, 455 East Grand Avenue, Chicago, Illinois. No commercial production is made from the deposit.

Platinum

The platinum-group metals occur in a very low ratio to the amount of gold in the placer mines, and only a small amount has been recovered in Siskiyou County. C. A. Logan (19) reported that the platinum-group metals are found in appreciable amounts only where serpentine and peridotite outcrop in the drainage basin of the placers. At the Michigan Salmon hydraulic mine, a few miles below Forks of Salmon, some almost pure osmiridium was recovered.

Yuba Consolidated Goldfields have recovered some platinum in their dredging operations on the Scott River below Callahan.

Pumice

Pumice is a very porous volcanic glass formed when great quantities of steam and other gases expand and escape from cooling molten lava. It occurs as a crust on lava flows and in beds where it was blown from erupting volcanoes. It often has a silky luster, and a cellular structure which makes it light enough to float on water. It is usually white or gray in color and has the composition of rhyolite or andesite. Scoria is a type of volcanic material formed from stiff basalt lavas and has larger holes more widely spaced than pumice.

The pumice deposits of Siskiyou County are located along the northern and eastern edges of the glass flow from Glass Mountain, and occur in horizontal beds some 14 feet thick at the edges of the flow, grading to about $2\frac{1}{2}$ feet thick a mile away. The pumice is fragmental, white to gray in color, and has an average maximum size of about 1 inch. Few pieces are over 2 inches in size.

Mining consists of stripping the surface of the beds free of shrubbery and forest litter with a bulldozer for an area about 100 feet square. Dump trucks of 5 to 7 cubic yards capacity are then loaded by a variety of apparatus including portable bucket elevators, dragline scrapers, power shovels, and from bins filled by bulldozers pushing the pumice over a ramp. The pumice when mined contains from 20 to 25 percent moisture and weighs about 1300 pounds per cubic yard. The railroad classifies it as a pumice scoria and has set a weight-equivalent of 1000 pounds to a cubic yard. It is hauled to sidings on the Great Northern Railroad at Tionesta and Ainshea Butte, where the bulk of it is loaded onto open gondola cars for shipment to west-coast cities. A small amount is shipped by truck to Klamath Falls processing plants, and some is made into building blocks at plants near Tionesta. Raw pumice sold for $2 per yard, and material ground to minus one-fourth-inch sold for $3 per yard on the cars at Tionesta in September 1946. Pumice bricks $3\frac{1}{2}$ by $3\frac{1}{2}$ by 6 inches in size are sawed from blocks of pumice broken from the crust of lava flows near the summit of Glass Mountain.

Fouch Claims. Roy Nial Fouch of Tionesta claimed about 900 acres of land on the north slope of Glass Mountain in secs. 22, 27, and 34, T. 44 N., R. 4 E., M. D. On the Christy claim in the SE¼ sec. 27, the pumice is about 14 feet deep above a sandy basalt. It is mined with a 1-cubic-yard slusher powered by a double-drum donkey hoist, chain-driven by a Chevrolet 6-cylinder automobile engine. The pumice is loaded into a 30-cubic-yard-capacity bin built of timbers, from which it can be loaded into trucks for hauling to the railroad, a distance of about 10 miles. In September 1946 Fouch was working alone at this property loading about a carload of pumice aggregate per day for C. V. Enloe, Jr., who was shipping from Ainshea Butte.

Glass Mountain Industries, owned by Charles P. von Doren, Box 648, Klamath Falls, Oregon, is a group of claims located on Glass Mountain in secs. 34, 35, T. 44 N., R. 4 E., M. D. A truck road has been built up the eastern slope of the mountain over the glass flow and obsidian boulders to an area where many of the obsidian boulders have a crust of pumice as much as 12 inches thick. Pumice boulders having the desired texture are sorted and loaded into trucks and hauled to Klamath Falls where they are sawed into scouring bricks.

Glass Mountain Volcolite Company. H. W. Free of Tionesta claims some 1720 acres in secs. 1 and 2, T. 43 N., R. 4 E., and secs. 25, 26, 34, 35, and 36, T. 44 N., R. 4 E., M. D. The bulk of his production has been used as aggregate in the manufacture of building blocks in his plant at Tionesta. Some scouring bricks have been produced from blocks mined on these claims.

John Madsen of Klamath Falls, Oregon, claims 280 acres of land in secs. 25, 26, and 35, T. 44 N., R. 4 E., M. D. A road cut near his cabin in the SW¼ sec. 26 opened a bed of pumice 10 feet deep, but there has been no production. Madsen has been sawing scouring bricks from pumice blocks mined in Modoc County.

Mount Hoffman pumice claims include 960 acres in sec. 28 and the E½ sec. 29, T. 44 N., R. 4 E., M.D. Some of the first pumice aggregate produced in Siskiyou County was mined from these claims in 1935 by E. L. Jamison, J. O. Miller, and Dan A. Williams. The property has been idle since 1942, but a ''desire to hold'' notice has been filed by Dan A. Williams, 217 Monterey Street, Salinas, California. (Averill 35, p. 335.)

Shasta Group. Twelve claims on the south slope of Cinder Cone Mountain in sec. 22, T. 42 N., R. 4 W., M.D., are owned by Clem and Nettie Baker of Yreka. Black volcanic cinders are mined from a pit about 300 feet long by backing a truck up to the slope and scooping the cinders into a trough slide to the truck. Very little of the material is over an inch in size. The depth of cinder deposit has not been determined, but the length is about 2000 feet. The cinders weigh 40 pounds per cubic foot and are used as a substitute for, or mixed with pumice as an aggregate in the manufacture of concrete blocks in building construction and as an insulation material.

Volcanic Products Corporation, Paul Dalton, manager, Williams Building, Klamath Falls, Oregon, owned and leased unpatented mining claims including 3411 acres near Glass Mountain in T. 44 N., R. 4 E., M.D., in 1937. Some of the claims were leased from the Christie estate, and others from R. N. Fouch of Klamath Falls, Oregon. Pumice of a maximum size of 1½ inches occurs in pits to a depth of 40 feet. It was mined by a five-eighths-cubic-yard Byers gasoline shovel and hauled to a crushing and screening plant at Leaf on the Southern Pacific Railroad. The plant included a set of rolls and a vibrating screen operated by an 80-horsepower Hercules gasoline engine. The product was sold for concrete aggregate.

Scoria boulders are found overlying the glass on the mountain, and they were sawed into scouring blocks on a 36-inch diameter circular saw having teeth faced with a hard alloy. A 12-inch carborundum-disc saw was used for trimming the bricks and a gang of five 16-inch-diameter mild-steel saws were used for sawing the bricks with powdered carborundum. A Dodge automobile engine furnished the power. Twenty-seven men were employed at the mine and six men at Leaf in July 1936. Production in 1936 amounted to 4000 cubic yards of pumice worth $14,000. f.o.b. railroad, and 15,000 pumice bricks 3 by 4 by 6 inches which sold for 10 cents each. No production has been reported by this company since 1938 and the properties they held are now operated by other interests.

Quicksilver

Great Northern quicksilver (Herzog-Morgan, Minnehaha, Empire Canyon Mining Company, Mercury) mine includes 15 quartz and 2 placer claims located in sec. 13, 14, and 24, T. 47 N., R. 8 W., M.D. J. C. Humphrey, legal owner, leased the property in March 1940 to C. N. White and C. W. Yates of Yreka. At an elevation 160 feet lower than the LeRoy level, a crosscut adit was driven N. 8° W. 455 feet to a vein 20 inches wide striking N. 20° E., and dipping 58° W. Native quicksilver and cinnabar occur in cracks and vugs in the brecciated vein filling. The vein was developed by drifting south for 150 feet and north 125 feet. Stopes about 30 feet long were worked above both drifts. The north drift was stoped 125 feet to the surface. The stope in the south drift was about 30 feet high and pinched out. A winze was sunk 60 feet deep below the LeRoy level at a point about 300 feet south of the adit. Ore from these developments, together with some of the gob from the old stopes, was sent to the new mill.

Ore was dumped from the mine cars through a 6-inch rail grizzly into two steel cylindrical ore bins, 8 feet in diameter and 24 feet high, equipped with steel gates. It was dropped from the bins through a 2- by 4-foot steel-slide grizzly with bars spaced at three-quarters of an inch. The oversize was crushed to 1½ inches in an 8- by 10-inch jaw crusher and joined the undersize on a belt-conveyor 14 inches wide and 77 feet long, which delivered it to a 12- by 12-foot steel cylindrical bin. This bin had a cone-shaped bottom fitted with an 8-inch pipe 4 feet long, which discharged the ore on the top hearth of a five-hearth, Nichols Herreshoff furnace. The furnace had a 10-foot-diameter steel shell lined with fire brick. Two rake arms revolved at 1 revolution per minute. Butane gas was mixed with air from a Victor-Acme type A.F. size 17 blower in two Hauck burners to provide heat at 1400 to 1450 degrees Fahrenheit. The furnace vapors were pulled through a Sirroco dust collector by a 24-inch fan which created a vacuum of 5 to 6 inches water-gage, and were delivered through a surge tank to two banks of condenser pipes. There were eleven cast-iron pipes, 8 inches in diameter by 18 feet in length, in each bank. They discharged under water into cast-iron pans. The quicksilver and sludge from the pan was mixed with lime in a sheet-iron box and the clean quicksilver weighed into flasks. The installation had a capacity of 24 tons per 24 hours.

Mine equipment included a Gardner-Denver 310-cubic-foot portable compressor, two jackhammers, and a stoper drill, together with accessory fittings and small tools.

The Empire Canyon Mining Company, Carl Yates, manager, succeeded White and Yates as operators in November 1941. In October 1942, B. W. Burtch of Seattle took over the operation and had some 16 men employed under Wm. S. Barquist, superintendent. After a short operation the plant was purchased by Edward F. Webber of Yreka who dismantled and sold the plant and equipment. (Averill 35, p. 336; Logan 25, pp. 495-496.)

Horse Creek Mercury. Small amounts of cinnabar occur in seams and cracks in a hornblende schist on the west bank of Horse Creek in secs. 15 and 16, T. 46 N., R. 10 W., M.D. It has been prospected by numerous short adits and shallow cuts, but no production has resulted. Cinnabar was recovered with the black sand in the dredging operations on Horse Creek but it was not retorted.

Sandstone

Sandstone beds outcropping in Shasta Valley were quarried and used in general construction prior to 1918. Many of the culverts on the Southern Pacific Railroad were built of sandstone. The following quarries were described in earlier reports of the Division of Mines.

Antone or *Weeks quarry* is 2 miles northeast of Yreka. The sandstone was quarried in layers from 6 inches to 8 feet thick and was used for building in Yreka. (Averill 35, p. 337.)

Fiock Brothers quarry is in sec. 13, T. 45 N., R. 7 W., M.D., near Yreka. The stone is coarse grained, even textured, and tawny in color. (Averill 35, p. 337.)

Southern Pacific Company has quarried considerable sandstone in sec. 29, T. 47 N., R. 6 W., M.D., near Hornbrook. This stone has been used for railroad culverts and for some buildings in Hornbrook. (Averill 35, p. 337.)

Silver

The silver produced in Siskiyou County has come as a by-product of gold and copper mining and amounts to about $260,000 in value.

Stone, Miscellaneous

Clements and Company of Hayward, California operated a gravel plant near Gazelle in sec. 10, T. 42 N., R. 6 W., M.D., on land owned by J. Robert Scott. The gravel was dug with a Northwest dragline equipped with a 40-foot boom and a three-fourths-cubic-yard bucket. It was crushed and screened to minus one-eighth-inch, mixed with oil in a Madsen No. 95 hot plant and used for building a stretch of Highway 99 north of Gazelle in June 1946.

Mount Shasta (Kottinger) gravel pit is located about 2 miles northwest of Mount Shasta in sec. 5, T. 40 N., R. 4 W., M.D., on ground owned by the McCloud River Railroad. The lease and equipment were purchased by J. S. Jensen and M. M. Thompson from A. E. Kottinger in August 1945. An andesitic gravel is dug to water level from pits about 25 feet deep. Equipment includes a P & H dragline with a 40-foot boom and a three-fourths-cubic-yard bucket; a Byres three-eighth-cubic-yard shovel; and a portable bucket line loader having 24 buckets 14 inches wide and 3 inches deep, chain driven from a Fordson tractor engine. Trucks are dumped into a hopper through a rail grizzly with 6-inch openings, and the gravel is fed into a jaw crusher set at 2 inches. The minus 2-inch material is lifted 40 feet with a bucket elevator to discharge over a triple-decked vibrating screen fitted with 1-inch, half-inch and quarter-inch screens. Sixty percent of the material is over a quarter of an inch in size and is classed as rock. Material that passes through a one-fourth-inch screen is classed as sand. Gravel is made up of half sand and half rock. Material over 1 inch in size is crushed in a Telesmith gyratory crusher and discharged over the vibrating screen from a bucket elevator. Most of the material is sold for concrete aggregate. Three men were employed at this pit in March 1947.

A. Young, South Highway 99, Yreka, loads sand and gravel from old dredge tailing piles on Greenhorn Creek, Yreka Creek, and from an old creek bottom about half a mile east of Gazelle, which he has leased from F. Foulke. The gravel is loaded with power shovels into dump trucks and hauled to his Yreka plant where it is crushed and screened to the desired sizes for use as concrete aggregate or for road construction.

BIBLIOGRAPHY

Allen, John Eliot

41 Geological investigation of the chromite deposits of California: California Div. Mines Rept. 37, pp. 101-167, 31 figs., 1941. (Siskiyou County, pp. 123-130.)

Aubury, Lewis E.

05 The copper resources of California: California Min. Bur. Bull. 23, 282 pp., illus., map, 1905. (Siskiyou County, pp. 102-111.)

08 The copper resources of California: California Min. Bur. Bull. 50, 366 pp., illus., maps, 1908. (Siskiyou County, pp. 120-133.)

Averill, Charles Volney

31 Redding field district—preliminary report on economic geology of the Shasta quadrangle: California Div. Mines Rept. 27, pp. 2-65, illus., 1931.

34 Redding field district—current mining development in northern California: California Div. Mines Rept. 30, pp. 303-309, 1934. (Siskiyou County, pp. 306-308.)

35 Redding field district—mines and mineral resources of Siskiyou County: California Div. Mines Rept. 31, pp. 255-338, illus., map, 1935.

38 Gold dredging in Shasta, Siskiyou, and Trinity Counties: California Div. Mines Rept. 34, pp. 96-126, illus., 1938.

46 Placer mining for gold in California: California Div. Mines Bull. 135, 377 pp., 4 pls., 106 figs., 1946. (Siskiyou County, pp. 293-303.)

Bradley, Walter W.

18 (et al.) Manganese and chromium in California: California Min. Bur. Bull. 76, 248 pp., illus., 1918.

Brown, G. Chester

16 Siskiyou County: California Min. Bur. Rept. 14, pp. 810-872, illus., 1916.

Crawford, J. J.

94 Twelfth report of the State Mineralogist, (second biennial), two years ending September 15, 1894: California Min. Bur. Rept. 12, 541 pp., illus., 1894.

96 Thirteenth report (third biennial) of the State Mineralogist for the two years ending September 15, 1896: California Min. Bur. Rept. 13, 726 pp., illus., 1896.

Diller, Joseph Silas

03 Klamath Mountain section, Cal.: Am. Jour. Sci., 4th ser., vol. 15, pp. 342-362, 1903.

14 Auriferous gravels in the Weaverville quadrangle, Cal.: U. S. Geol. Survey Bull. 540, pp. 11-21, map, 1914.

Dunn, R. L.

93 Siskiyou County: California Min. Bur. Rept. 11, pp. 420-449, 1893.

Haley, Charles Scott

23 Gold placers of California: California Min. Bur. Bull. 92, 167 pp., illus., maps, 1923.

Hamilton, Fletcher

22   A review of mining in California during 1921 with notes on the outlook for 1922: California Min. Bur. Preliminary Rept. 8, 68 pp., 1922.

Hershey, Oscar H.

01   Metamorphic formations of northwestern California: Am. Geologist, vol. 27, pp. 225-245, 1901.

12   The Belt and Pelona series: Am. Jour. Sci., 4th ser., vol. 34, pp. 263-273, 1912.

Hobson, J. B.

90   Siskiyou County: California Min. Bur. Rept. 10, pp. 655-658, 1890.

Irelan, William Jr.

88   Eighth annual report of the State Mineralogist for the year ending October 1, 1888: California Min. Bur. Rept. 8, 948 pp., illus., 1888. (Siskiyou County, pp. 581-631.)

Jenkins, Olaf P.

35   New technique applicable to the study of placers: California Div. Mines Rept. 31, pp. 143-210, pl. 3, 34 figs., 1935.

38   Geologic map of California, scale 1:500,000, California Div. Mines, 1938.

Laizure, C. McK

21   Siskiyou County: California Min. Bur. Rept. 17, pp. 529-536, 1921.

Logan, Clarence A.

19   Platinum and allied metals in California: California Min. Bur. Bull. 85, 120 pp., illus., 1919.

25   Sacramento field division—Siskiyou County: California Min. Bur. Rept. 21, pp. 413-498, illus., 1925.

Maxson, John H.

33   Economic geology of portions of Del Norte and Siskiyou Counties, north-westernmost California: California Div. Mines Rept. 29, pp. 123-160, 26 figs., map, 1933.

O'Brien, J. C.

43   Current notes on activity in the strategic minerals, Redding field district: California Div. Mines Rept. 39, pp. 77-84, 1943. (Siskiyou County, pp. 82-83.)

43a   Current notes on the activity in the strategic minerals, Redding field district: California Div. Mines Rept. 39, pp. 323-330, 1943. (Siskiyou County, pp. 327-329.)

Trask, Parker D.

43   (**Wilson, I. F.**, and **Simons, F. S.**)   Manganese deposits of California— a summary report: California Div. Mines Bull. 125, pp. 51-215, 2 figs., map, 1943. (Siskiyou County, pp. 88, 183-185.)

Tucker, W. Burling

22   Redding field division: California Min. Bur. Rept. 18, pp. 295-298, 1922. (Siskiyou County, pp. 297-298.)

22a   Redding field division: California Min. Bur. Rept. 18, pp. 595-601, illus., 1922. (Siskiyou County, p. 600.)

22b   Redding field division: California Min. Bur. Rept. 18, pp. 729, 736, illus., 1922. (Siskiyou County, p. 733.)

23   Redding field division—review of mining during 1922: California Min. Bur. Rept. 19, pp. 7-13, 1923.

23a   Redding field division: California Min. Bur. Rept. 19, pp. 135-140, 1923. (Siskiyou County, pp. 138-139.)

23b   Redding field division: California Min. Bur. Rept. 19, pp. 55-59, 1923. (Siskiyou County, p. 58.)

United States Geological Survey

43   Department of the Interior information service: California Div. Mines Rept. 39, pp. 90-102, 1943. (Chromite deposits of McGuffy Creek area, Siskiyou County, California, pp. 92-94; The Fairview and Ladd chromite deposits, Siskiyou County, California, pp. 94-96.)

Waring, G. A.

15   Springs of California: U. S. Geol. Survey Water-Supply Paper 338, 410 pp., 13 pls., 1915.

Watts, W. L.

93   Mineral springs in Siskiyou County: California Min. Bur. Rept. 11, pp. 449-452, 1893.

www.GoldMiningBooks.com

Books On Mining

Visit: www.goldminingbooks.com to order your copies or ask your favorite book seller or mining shop to offer them.

Note: Wholesale copies are available at 50% of listed cover price.

Mining Books by Kerby Jackson

Gold Dust: Stories From Oregon's Mining Years - Oregon mining historian and prospector, Kerby Jackson, brings you a treasure trove of seventeen stories on Southern Oregon's rich history of gold prospecting, the prospectors and their discoveries, and the breathtaking areas they settled in and made homes. 5" X 8", 98 ppgs. Retail Price: $11.99

The Golden Trail: More Stories From Oregon's Mining Years - In his follow-up to "Gold Dust: Stories of Oregon's Mining Years", this time around, Jackson brings us twelve tales from Oregon's Gold Rush, including the story about the first gold strike on Canyon Creek in Grant County, about the old timers who found gold by the pail full at the Victor Mine near Galice, how Iradel Bray discovered a rich ledge of gold on the Coquille River during the height of the Rogue River War, a tale of two elderly miners on the hunt for a lost mine in the Cascade Mountains, details about the discovery of the famous Armstrong Nugget and others. 5" X 8", 70 ppgs. Retail Price: $10.99

Alaska Mining Books

Ore Deposits of the Willow Creek Mining District, Alaska - Unavailable since 1954, this hard to find publication includes valuable insights into the Willow Creek Mining District near Hatcher Pass in Alaska. The publication includes insights into the history, geology and locations of the well known mines in the area, including the Gold Cord, Independence, Fern, Mabel, Lonesome, Snowbird, Schroff-O'Neil, High Grade, Marion Twin, Thorpe, Webfoot, Kelly-Willow, Lane, Holland and others. 8.5" X 11", 96 ppgs. Retail Price: $9.99

The Juneau Gold Belt of Alaska - Unavailable since 1906, this hard to find publication includes valuable insights into the gold mines around Juneau, Alaska. The publication includes important details into the history, geology and locations of the well known gold mines and prospects in the area, including those around Windham Bay, Holkham Bay, Port Snettisham, on Grindstone and Rhine Creeks, Gold Creek, Douglas Island, Salmon Creek, Lemon Creek, Nugget Creek, from the Mendenhall River to Berners Bay, McGinnis Creek, Montana Creek, Peterson Creek, Windfall Creek, the Eagle River, Yankee Basin, Yankee Curve, Kowee Creek and elsewhere. Not only are gold placer mines included, but also hardrock gold mines. 8.5" X 11", 224 ppgs. Retail Price: $19.99

Mining in the Jumbo Basin of Alaska - Unavailable since 1953, this hard to find publication includes valuable insights into the mines and geology of the Jumbo Basin. The publication includes important details into the history, geology and locations of the well known gold mines and prospects in the famous Jumbo Basin Mining Region of Alaska.
72 ppgs, 9.99

The Rampart Placer Gold Region of Alaska - Unavailable since 1906, this hard to find publication includes valuable insights into the placer gold mines of the Rampart Mining Region. The publication includes important details into the history, geology and locations of the well known gold mines and prospects in the famous Rampart Mining Region of Alaska.
78 ppgs, 10.99

Arizona Mining Books

Mines and Mining in Northern Yuma County Arizona - Originally published in 1911, this important publication on Arizona Mining has not been available for over a hundred years. Included are rare insights into the gold, silver, copper and quicksilver mines of Yuma County, Arizona together with hard to find maps and photographs. Some of the mines and mining districts featured include the Planet Copper Mine, Mineral Hill, the Clara Consolidated Mine, Viati Mine, Copper Basin prospect, Bowman Mine, Quartz King, Billy Mack, Carnation, the Wardwell and Osbourne, Valensuella Copper, the Mariquita, Colonial Mine, the French American, the New York-Plomosa, Guadalupe, Lead Camp, Mudersbach Copper Camp, Yellow Bird, the Arizona Northern (Salome Strike), Bonanza (Harqua Hala), Golden Eagle, Hercules, Socorro and others. **8.5" X 11", 144 ppgs. Retail Price: $11.99**

The Aravaipa and Stanley Mining Districts of Graham County Arizona - Originally published in 1925, this important publication on Arizona Mining has not been available for nearly ninety years. Included are rare insights into the gold and silver mines of these two important mining districts, together with hard to find maps. **8.5" X 11", 140 ppgs. Retail Price: $11.99**

Gold in the Gold Basin and Lost Basin Mining Districts of Mohave County, Arizona - This volume contains rare insights into the geology and gold mineralization of the Gold Basin and Lost Basin Mining Districts of Mohave County, Arizona that will be of benefit to miners and prospectors. Also included is a significant body of information on the gold mines and prospects of this portion of Arizona. This volume is lavishly illustrated with rare photos and mining maps. **8.5" X 11", 188 ppgs. Retail Price: $19.99**

Mines of the Jerome and Bradshaw Mountains of Arizona - This important publication on Arizona Mining has not been available for ninety years. This volume contains rare insights into the geology and ore deposits of the Jerome and Bradshaw Mountains of Arizona that will be of benefit to miners and prospectors who work those areas. Included is a significant body of information on the mines and prospects of the Verde, Black Hills, Cherry Creek, Prescott, Walker, Groom Creek, Hassayampa, Bigbug, Turkey Creek, Agua Fria, Black Canyon, Peck, Tiger, Pine Grove, Bradshaw, Tintop, Humbug and Castle Creek Mining Districts. This volume is lavishly illustrated with rare photos and mining maps. **8.5" X 11", 218 ppgs. Retail Price: $19.99**

The Ajo Mining District of Pima County Arizona - This important publication on Arizona Mining has not been available for nearly seventy years. This volume contains rare insights into the geology and mineralization of the Ajo Mining District in Pima County, Arizona and in particular the famous New Cornelia Mine. **8.5" X 11", 126 ppgs. Retail Price: $11.99**

Mining in the Santa Rita and Patagonia Mountains of Arizona - Originally published in 1915, this important publication on Arizona Mining has not been available for nearly a century. Included are rare insights into hundreds of gold, silver, copper and other mines in this famous Arizona mining area. Details include the locations, geology, history, production and other facts of the mines of this region. **8.5" X 11", 394 ppgs. Retail Price: $24.99**

Mining in the Bisbee Quadrangle of Arizona - Originally published in 1906, this important publication on Arizona Mining has not been available for nearly a century. Included are rare insights into hundreds of gold, silver, copper and other mines in this famous Arizona mining area. Details include the locations, geology, history, production and other facts of the mines of this important mining region. **8.5" X 11", 188 ppgs. Retail Price: $14.99**

Placer Gold Mining in Arizona - Unavailable since 1922, this hard to find publication includes valuable insights into the placer gold mines of the Arizona. Originally released as "Placer Gold of Arizona", despite its small size, this publication includes important details into the history, geology and locations of the well known placer gold mines and prospects in the State of Arizona. **48 ppgs, 8.99**

Gold and Copper Mining near Payson, Arizona - Written in 1915, this hard to find publication includes valuable insights into the gold and copper mining industry of Arizona. Highlighted here are the gold and copper mines near Payson, Arizona. **68 ppgs, 8.99**

Lode Gold Mining in Arizona - Unavailable since 1934, this hard to find publication, originally released as "Arizona Lode Gold Mines and Gold Mining" includes valuable insights into the gold mining industry of Arizona. Included are valuable insights into over 150 hardrock gold mines in over 30 different mining districts in Arizona. **278 ppgs, 21.99**

Mining in the Dragoon Quadrangle of Cochise County, Arizona - Unavailable since 1964, this hard to find publication includes valuable insights into the mines of the Dragoon Quadrangle Mining Region. The publication includes important details into the history, geology and locations of the well known mines and prospects in this famous mining region of Arizona. **224 ppgs., 19.99**

Directory of Operating Mines in Arizona in 1915 - Unavailable since 1916, this hard to find publication includes valuable insights into the mines of Arizona. This small publication includes a complete list of the mines that were operating in the State of Arizona during 1915 and includes details such as general location, owners and some basic facts about each mining operation. **52 ppgs. 8.99**

Arizona Ore Deposits - Unavailable since 1938, this hard to find publication includes valuable insights into some ore deposits of Arizona. Included are valuable insights into the formation and characteristics of valuable ore deposits in the Jerome, Miami, Inspiration, Clifton, Morenci, Ray, Ajo, Eureka, Tombstone and Magma mining districts. Included are details into some of the major gold, silver and copper mines of these important Arizona mining areas. 160 ppgs, 14.99

Mining in Santa Cruz County, Arizona - Written in 1916, this hard to find publication includes valuable facts on the mines of this famous mining area, which is the oldest in Arizona. Included in this small booklet are hard to find details on the history and mines and prospects of this area. 54 ppgs, 7.99

The Mineral Industries of Arizona: A Brief History of the Development of Arizona's Mineral Resources - Written in 1962, this hard to find publication includes valuable facts about the Arizona mining industry. Included in this small booklet is a brief history of gold, silver and copper mining in Arizona. 54 ppgs, 7.99

Mining in Southern Yuma County, Arizona - Written in 1933, this hard to find publication includes valuable facts on the gold, silver and copper mines of this famous mining area. Included are the hard to find locations, histories and details of numerous mines in Yuma County, including the Silver Clip, Amelia, Revelation,Mendevil, Chloride, Cash Entry, Mandarin, Saxon, Princess, Hamburg, Silver King, Geronimo, Red Cloud, Black Rock, Pacific, Mandan, Silver Glance, Papago, Riverview, Hardt, Broadway, Jupiter, Annie, Flora Temple, Senora, Castle Dome, New Dil, Lady Edith, Big Dome, Yuma, Little Dome, Hull, Cleveland-Chicago, Adams, Mabel, Lincoln, Big Eye, Sheep, Keystone, King of Arizona, North Dstar, Geyser, Rand, IXL, Regal, C.O.D., Big Horn, Cemitosa, Alamo, Alnoah, Tunnel Springs, and dozens of others. 262 ppgs., 20.99

Geology of the San Manuel Copper Deposit of Arizona - Written in 1951, this hard to find publication includes valuable facts about this important copper mining area in Pinal County, Arizona. 98 ppgs, 9.99

Mining in the Sierrita Mountains of Pima County, Arizona - Written in 1921, this hard to find publication includes valuable facts on the mines of this famous mining area in Pima County. Included in this small booklet are hard to find details on the history and mines and prospects of this area. 54 ppgs, 8.99

Mining in the Cerbat Range, Black Mountains and Grand Wash Cliffs: Mohave County, Arizona - Written in 1909, this hard to find publication includes valuable facts on the Mines and Mineral Deposits in the Cerbat Range, Black Mountains and Grand Wash Cliffs of Mohave County, Arizona. Included are the hard to find locations and details on dozens of gold, silver and copper mines in this famous Arizona mining region. 254 ppgs, 24.99

Uranium Mining at the Dripping Spring Quartzite in Gila County, Arizona - Written in 1969, this hard to find publication includes valuable facts on the Mines and Mineral Deposits in the uranium mining area of Dripping Spring in Gila County, Arizona. Included are the hard to find locations, details and maps of uranium deposits in Gila County. 136 ppgs, 12.99

Arizona Gold Placers - Written in 1927, this hard to find publication includes valuable insights into the gold placer deposits of Arizona. Highlighted here are the details you need to find placer gold in Arizona, including the location of Arizona placer gold mines. 92 ppgs, 8.99

Geology of the Lower Gila Region of Arizona - Written in 1921, this hard to find publication includes valuable facts on the geology in Gila County, Arizona. Included in this small booklet are hard to find details on the geology of this area that will be of aid to prospectors, miners, rock hounds and geologic students. 46 ppgs, 7.99

The Wallapai Mining District of Mohave County, Arizona - Written in 1951, this hard to find publication includes valuable facts on the mines of this famous mining area in the Cerbat Mountains. Included in this small booklet are hard to find details on the history and mines and prospects of this area. 68 ppgs, 8.99

California Mining Books

The Tertiary Gravels of the Sierra Nevada of California - Mining historian Kerby Jackson introduces us to a classic mining work by Waldemar Lindgren in this important re-issue of The Tertiary Gravels of the Sierra Nevada of California. Unavailable since 1911, this publication includes details on the gold bearing ancient river channels of the famous Sierra Nevada region of California. 8.5" X 11", 282 ppgs. Retail Price: $19.99

The Mother Lode Mining Region of California - Unavailable since 1900, this publication includes details on the gold mines of California's famous Mother Lode gold mining area. Included are details on the geology, history and important gold mines of the region, as well as insights into historic mining methods, mine timbering, mining machinery, mining bell signals and other details on how these mines operated. Also included are insights into the gold mines of the California Mother Lode that were in operation during the first sixty years of California's mining history. 8.5" X 11", 176 ppgs. Retail Price: $14.99

Lode Gold of the Klamath Mountains of Northern California and South West Oregon - Unavailable since 1971, this publication was originally compiled by Preston E. Hotz and includes details on the lode mining districts of Oregon and California's Klamath Mountains. Included are details on the geology, history and important lode mines of the French Gulch, Deadwood, Whiskeytown, Shasta, Redding, Muletown, South Fork, Old Diggings, Dog Creek (Delta), Bully Choop (Indian Creek), Harrison Gulch, Hayfork, Minersville, Trinity Center, Canyon Creek, East Fork, New River, Denny, Liberty (Black Bear), Cecilville, Callahan, Yreka, Fort Jones and Happy Camp mining districts in California, as well as the Ashland, Rogue River, Applegate, Illinois River, Takilma, Greenback, Galice, Silver Peak, Myrtle Creek and Mule Creek districts of South Western Oregon. Also included are insights into the mineralization and other characteristics of this important mining region. **8.5" X 11", 100 ppgs. Retail Price: $10.99**

Mines and Mineral Resources of Shasta County, Siskiyou County, Trinity County: California - Unavailable since 1915, this publication was originally compiled by the California State Mining Bureau and includes details on the gold mines of this area of Northern California. Also included are insights into the mineralization and other characteristics of this important mining region, as well as the location of historic gold mines. **8.5" X 11", 204 ppgs. Retail Price: $19.99**

Geology of the Yreka Quadrangle, Siskiyou County, California - Unavailable since 1977, this publication was originally compiled by Preston E. Hotz and includes details on the geology of the Yreka Quadrangle of Siskiyou County, California. Also included are insights into the mineralization and other characteristics of this important mining region. **8.5" X 11", 78 ppgs. Retail Price: $7.99**

Mines of San Diego and Imperial Counties, California - Originally published in 1914, this important publication on California Mining has not been available for a century. This publication includes important information on the early gold mines of San Diego and Imperial County, which were some of the first gold fields mined in California by early Spanish and Mexican miners before the 49ers came on the scene. Included are not only details on early mining methods in the area, production statistics and geological information, but also the location of the early gold mines that helped make California "The Golden State". Also included are details on the mining of other minerals such as silver, lead, zinc, manganese, tungsten, vanadium, asbestos, barite, borax, cement, clay, dolomite, fluospar, gem stones, graphite, marble, salines, petroleum, stronium, talc and others. **8.5" X 11", 116 ppgs. Retail Price: $12.99**

Mines of Sierra County, California - Unavailable since 1920, this publication was originally compiled by the California State Mining Bureau and includes details on the gold mines of Sierra County, California. Also included are insights into the mineralization and other characteristics of this important mining region, as well as the location of historic gold mines. **8.5" X 11", 156 ppgs. Retail Price: $19.99**

Mines of Plumas County, California - Unavailable since 1918, this publication was originally compiled by the California State Mining Bureau and includes details on the gold mines of Plumas County, California. Also included are insights into the mineralization and other characteristics of this important mining region, as well as the location of historic gold mines. **8.5" X 11", 200 ppgs. Retail Price: $19.99**

Mines of El Dorado, Placer, Sacramento and Yuba Counties, California - Originally published in 1917, this important publication on California Mining has not been available for nearly a century. This publication includes important information on the early gold mines of El Dorado County, Placer County, Sacramento County and Yuba County, which were some of the first gold fields mined by the Forty-Niners during the California Gold Rush. Included are not only details on early mining methods in the area, production statistics and geological information, but also the location of the early gold mines that helped make California "The Golden State". Also included are insights into the early mining of chrome, copper and other minerals in this important mining area. **8.5" X 11", 204 ppgs. Retail Price: $19.99**

Mines of Los Angeles, Orange and Riverside Counties, California - Originally published in 1917, this important publication on California Mining has not been available for nearly a century. This publication includes important information on the early gold mines of Los Angeles County, Orange County and Riverside County, which were some of the first gold fields mined in California by early Spanish and Mexican miners before the 49ers came on the scene. Included are not only details on early mining methods in the area, production statistics and geological information, but also the location of the early gold mines that helped make California "The Golden State". **8.5" X 11", 146 ppgs. Retail Price: $12.99**

Mines of San Bernadino and Tulare Counties, California - From 1917, this publication on California Mining has not been available for nearly a century. This publication includes important information on the early gold mines of San Bernadino and Tulare County, which were some of the first gold fields mined in California by early Spanish and Mexican miners before the 49ers came on the scene. Included are not only details on early mining methods in the area, production statistics and geological information, but also the location of the early gold mines that helped make California "The Golden State". Also included are details on the mining of other minerals such as copper, iron, lead, zinc, manganese, tungsten, vanadium, asbestos, barite, borax, cement, clay, dolomite, fluospar, gem stones, graphite, marble, salines, petroleum, stronium, talc and others. **8.5" X 11", 200 ppgs. Retail Price: $19.99**

Chromite Mining in The Klamath Mountains of California and Oregon - Unavailable since 1919, this publication was originally compiled by J.S. Diller of the United States Department of Geological Survey and includes details on the chromite mines of this area of Northern California and Southern Oregon. Also included are insights into the mineralization and other characteristics of this important mining region, as well as the location of historic mines. Also included are insights into chromite mining in Eastern Oregon and Montana. **8.5" X 11", 98 ppgs. Retail Price: $9.99**

Mines and Mining in Amador, Calaveras and Tuolumne Counties, California - Unavailable since 1915, this publication was originally compiled by William Tucker and includes details on the mines and mineral resources of this important California mining area. Included are details on the geology, history and important gold mines of the region, as well as insights into other local mineral resources such as asbestos, clay, copper, talc, limestone and others. Also included are insights into the mineralization and other characteristics of this important portion of California's Mother Lode mining region. **8.5" X 11", 198 ppgs. Retail Price: $14.99**

The Cerro Gordo Mining District of Inyo County California - Unavailable since 1963, this publication was originally compiled by the United States Department of Interior. Included are insights into the mineralization and other characteristics of this important mining region of Southern California. Topics include the mining of gold and silver in this important mining district in Inyo County, California, including details on the history, production and locations of the Cerro Gordo Mine, the Morning Star Mine, Estelle Tunnel, Charles Lease Tunnel, Ignacio, Hart, Crosscut Tunnel, Sunset, Upper Newtown, Newtown, Ella, Perseverance, Newsboy, Belmont and other silver and gold mines in the Cerro Gordo Mining District. This volume also includes important insights into the fossil record, geologic formations, faults and other aspects of economic geology in this California mining district. **8.5" X 11", 104 ppgs. Retail Price: $10.99**

Mining in Butte, Lassen, Modoc, Sutter and Tehama Counties of California - Unavailable since 1917, this publication was originally compiled by the United States Department of Interior. Included are insights into the mineralization and other characteristics of this important mining region of California. Topics include the mining of asbestos, chromite, gold, diamonds and manganese in Butte County, the mining of gold and copper in the Hayden Hill and Diamond Mountain mining districts of Lassen County, the mining of coal, salt, copper and gold in the High Grade and Winters mining districts of Modoc County, gold mining in Sutter County and the mining of gold, chromite, manganese and copper in Tehama County. This volume also includes the production records and locations of numerous mines in this important mining region. **8.5" X 11", 114 ppgs. Retail Price: $11.99**

Mines of Trinity County California - Originally published in 1965, this important publication on California Mining has not been available for nearly fifty years. This publication includes important information on mines and mining in Trinity County, California, as well insights into the mineralization and geology of this important mining area in Northern California. Included are extensive details on hardrock and placer gold mines and prospects, including charts showing the locations of these historic mines.. **8.5" X 11", 144 ppgs. Retail Price: $12.99**

Mines of Kern County California - Originally published in 1962, this important publication on California Mining has not been available for nearly fifty years. This publication includes important information on mines and mining in Kern County, California, as well insights into the mineralization and geology of this important mining area in California. Included are extensive details on hardrock and placer gold mines and prospects, including charts showing the locations of these historic mines. **8.5" X 11", 398 ppgs. Retail Price: $24.99**

Mines of Calaveras County California - Originally published in 1962, this important publication on California Mining has not been available for nearly fifty years. This publication includes important information on mines and mining in Calaveras County, California, as well insights into the mineralization and geology of this important mining area in Northern California. Included are extensive details on hardrock and placer gold mines and prospects, including charts showing the locations of these historic mines. **8.5" X 11", 236 ppgs. Retail Price: $19.99**

Lode Gold Mining in Grass Valley California - Unavailable since 1940, this publication was originally compiled by the United States Department of Interior. Included are insights into the gold mineralization and other characteristics of this important mining region of Nevada County, California. This volume also includes important insights into the geologic formations, faults and other aspects of economic geology in this California mining district. Of particular interest are the fine details on many hardrock gold mines in the area, including their locations, histories, development and mineralization. Some of the mines featured include the Gold Hill Mine, Massachusetts Hill, Boundary, Peabody, Golden Center, North Star, Omaha, Lone Jack, Homeward Bound, Hartery, Wisconsin, Allison Ranch, Phoenix, Kate Hayes, W.Y.O.D., Empire, Rich Hill, Daisy Hill, Orleans, Sultana, Centennial, Conlin, Ben Franklin, Crown Point and many others. **8.5" X 11", 148 ppgs. Retail Price: $12.99**

Lode Mining in the Alleghany District of Sierra County California - Unavailable since 1913, this publication was originally compiled by the United States Department of Interior. Included are insights into the mineralization and other characteristics of this important mining region of Sierra County. Included are details on the history, production and locations of numerous hardrock gold mines in this famous California area, including the Tightner Mine, Minnie D., Osceola, Eldorado, Twenty One, Sherman, Kenton, Oriental, Rainbow, Plumbago, Irelan, Gold Canyon, North Fork, Federal, Kate Hardy and others. This volume also includes important insights into the fossil record, geologic formations, faults and other aspects of economic geology in this California mining district. **8.5" X 11", 48 ppgs.** Retail Price: $7.99

Six Months In The Gold Mines During The California Gold Rush - Unavailable since 1850, this important work is a first hand account of one "49'ers" personal experience during the great California Gold Rush, shedding important light on one of the most exciting periods in the history of not only California, but also the world. Compiled from journals written between 1847 and 1849 by E. Gould Buffum, a native of New York, "Six Months In The Gold Mines During The California Gold Rush" offers a rare look into the day to day lives of the people who came to California to work in her gold mines when the state was still a great frontier. **8.5" X 11", 290 ppgs.** Retail Price: $19.99

Quartz Mines of the Grass Valley Mining District of California - Unavailable since 1867, this important publication has not been available since those days. This rare publication offers a short dissertation on the early hardrock mines in this important mining district in the California Mother Lode region between the 1850's and 1860's. Also included are hard to find details on the mineralization and locations of these mines, as well as how they were operated in those day. **8.5" X 11", 44 ppgs.** Retail Price: $8.99

Gold Rush on the Feather River - First published in 1924, this short publication by G.C. Mansfield sheds important light on the early history of gold mining on the Feather River. Included are rare insights into the first decade of gold mining and the early mining camps of the Feather River during the 1850's. **64 ppgs., 9.99**

The Bodie Mining District of California - First published in 1986, it has been unavailable since those days and sheds important light on this famous mining area. Included are the history, characteristics and locations of numerous old mines around the ghost town of Bodie. **64 ppgs, 8.99**

Geology and Mineral Resources of the Gasquet Quadrangle of California-Oregon - First published in 1953, it has been unavailable for over a century and sheds important light on the geological features and mineral resources of this portion of Northern California and Southern Oregon. **80 ppgs, 9.99**

Gold Dredging in California - Unavailable since 1905, this publication was originally compiled by the California Bureau of Mines. A century and more ago, giant dredging machines dug in California's rivers and creeks in search of illusive golden riches. First appearing in the 1850's, gold dredges finally reached their peak of development in Siberia and New Zealand before becoming popular again in the United States. This book offers a unique historical perspective on the gold dredges that once operated in California. This book on California mining history is lavishly illustrated with dozens of rare historic photos gold dredges that once operated in California, as well as hard to locate plans on how these dredges were designed. **148 ppgs, 12.99**

Gold Placer Mining in California - Unavailable since 1923, this publication was originally compiled by the California Bureau of Mines. Included are insights into the history of placer gold mining in California, ranging from using a simple gold pan, rocker box or sluice box, right up to the largest of hydraulic mines. All of the major placer gold mining areas are covered in detail, complete with the methods that were used to mine them. This hard to find, previously out of print publication will offer valuable insights for those who are looking for gold and other valuable minerals in California or to those who are interested in mining history. **194 ppgs, 19.99**

The Mother Lode Gold System of California - Unavailable since 1929, this publication offers rare insights into the famous Mother Lode Mining Region of California. Included are facts about the local geology, ore deposits, ore genesis and the important gold mines of this important mining area in the California Mother Lode. Includes hard to find details and locations of dozens of hard rock gold mines in the area. This hard to find, previously out of print publication will offer valuable insights for those who are looking for gold and other valuable minerals in California's Mother Lode and surrounding areas, or those who are interested in mining history. **11.99, 132 ppgs**

Mines and Minerals of California - Unavailable since 1899, this publication offers rare insights into the early mining industry of California. Included are facts about the early mining history of California, including details on the State's famous gold mining areas, quicksilver mining, copper mining and the early California petroleum industry. This hard to find, previously out of print publication will offer valuable insights for those who are looking for gold or other minerals in California or those who are interested in mining history. **24.99, 458 ppgs**

California Golden Treasures: Placer Gold Mining in California in the 1850's - "The Autobiography of Charles Peters: The Good Luck Days of Placer Mining in the 1850's". It was first published in 1915, and later reprinted under the title of "California Golden Treasures", but few copies remain available today. In 1915, Charles Peters was "the oldest pioneer living in California, who mined in ... the days of '49". He was born in Portugal in 1825, first visited California in 1846 as a merchant seaman and returned three years later to seek gold at Columbia, Jackson Creek, and Mokelumne Hill. "California Golden Treasures" is the memoir of his life through the 1850s, followed by a series of "Good Luck" stories, miscellaneous tales of the mining camps, a few of which seem to be credited to Peters, although most were actually the work of another author, drawn from many sources. Also included are many historical happenings, interesting incidents and illustrations of the old mining towns in the good luck era, the placer mining days of the '50s. 19.99, 262 ppgs

Gemstones of California - First published in 1905 as "Gems, Jeweler's Materials and Ornamental Stones of California", it has been unavailable since those days and sheds important light on the gems and precious stones that may be found in California. Included are chapters on diamonds, corundum, topaz, spinel, beryl, garnet, tourmaline, quartz, chalcedony, chrysoprase, jasper, opal, albite, orthoclase, labrodite, jade, lapis lazuli, epidote, apatite, fluorite, hematite, azurite, malachite, turquoise, amber, cat's-eye, pearl, abalone and many others. Included are details on where these gems and precious stones may be found in California, as well as their characteristics. Also included is a chapter on California's gem mines. 15.99, 198 ppgs

Placer Mining For Gold In California - Unavailable since 1946, this publication offers rare insights into the early mining industry of California. Included are facts about the various historical methods of placer mining utilized in California, as well as critical insights into how and where to find placer gold in California. This hard to find, previously out of print publication will offer valuable insights for those who are looking for gold in California, whether they are just starting out or whether they consider themselves an old hand at it. Quite possibly the most informative book available on the subject of placer gold mining. 24.99, 384 ppgs

Butte County, California: Its Advantages and Resources - Mining historian Kerby Jackson introduces us to a classic work of California history in this important re-issue of "Butte County Its Resources and Advantages" which was written by the Rev. Jesse Wood in 1888. This short booklet informs the reader about the early development and resources of Butte County, California. The booklet offers a unique look at Butte County's early communities and their industries in the late 19th century. 12.99, 108 ppgs

What Butte County Offers The Homeseeker - Mining historian Kerby Jackson introduces us to a classic work of California history in this important re-issue of "What Butte County Offers the Homeseeker" which was written by George C. Mansfield and Walter M. Smith in 1919. This short booklet informs the reader about the early development and resources of Butte County, California and the opportunities that were available to those interested in locating to the area just after World War One. The booklet offers a unique look at Butte County's early communities and their industries, namely gold mining and agriculture. 9.99, 68 ppgs

Butte: The Story of a California County - Mining historian Kerby Jackson introduces us to a classic work of California history in this important re-issue of "Butte: The Story of a California County" which was written by George C. Mansfield in 1919. This hard to find booklet tells the story of how Butte County, California first came into existence, starting with details about its first native inhabitants who lived there before the coming of the white man and his first settlements which was a result of the 1849 California Gold Rush. It goes on to discuss the lives of the first settlers, rounding them out with details about their quest for gold in what became Butte County. Also featured are details on early towns in the county, how they were governed and how their early occupants did their work and spent their leisure time. 9.99, 68 ppgs

The History of Butte County, California: In Two Volumes - Mining historian Kerby Jackson introduces us to a classic work of California history in this important re-issue of "The History of Butte County, California: In Two Volumes" which was written by Harry Laurenz Wells, Frank Gilbert and W.L. Chambers in 1882. This hard to find publication consists of two major parts. The first is a 126 page history of the early settlement of California from 1513 to 1850. The second portion is a history of Butte County from its earliest days of settlement to the early 1880. Chapter topics in the first section include Discovery of and Failure to Occupy California by Spain, Occupation of Lower California by the Jesuits, Conquest of Upper California by the Franciscans, Downfall of the Missions, Spanish Military Occupation, California as a Mexican Territory, The Bear Flag War, The Flores Insurrection, California Admitted to the Union, The Great Fur Companies and their Trapping Expeditions, Settlement of the Sacramento Valley and The Discovery of Gold in California. Chapter topics in the second part, include the Organization of Butte County, Its Early History, Changes in County Boundaries, Formation of Townships, Butte County's County Seat and Courthouse, Butte County Hospital and Infirmary, Elections and County Officers, A History of Crime in Butte County, A History of the Bench and Bar, Press of Butte County, Navigation on the Sacramento River, County Stage Routes, Butte County Agriculture, Butte County's Mining Industry and Indian Difficulties. Also included are details on local communities in Butte County such as Chico City, Oroville, Nord, Anita, Cana, Biggs, Gridley, Nelson, Durham, Dayton, Oregon City, Cherokee, Pence's Ranch, Magalia or Dogtown, Concow Township, Yankee Hill, Concow Valley, Bidwell's Bar, Hamilton, Thompson's Flat, Powellton, Inskip, Lovelocks, Stringtown, Enterprise, Forbestown, Clipper Mills, Bangor, Wyandotte, Boston Ranch or Hurlton and others, many of which are now considered ghost towns.

Also included are insights into the geology of the county and a history of local churches and schools. Also included are the biographies of 42 early settlers in Butte County, Caliornia. This text is heavily illustrated with 50 plus plates depicting important figures in California history, as well as various historic locations in Butte County.   24.99, 366 ppgs

Sights in the Gold Region of Oregon and California - Unavailable since 1853, this publication provides a fascinating insight into the California and Oregon Gold Rushes through the eyes of one of the men who went West and "saw the elephant" to take part in it. Theodore Taylor Johnson's memoir of his journey to the gold fields of California and Oregon offers a unique look into this important time during the settling of the Far West.   382 ppgs, 24.99

Colorado Mining Books

Ores of The Leadville Mining District - Unavailable since 1926, this publication was originally compiled by the United States Department of Interior. This volume also includes important insights into the ores and mineralization of the Leadville Mining District in Colorado. Topics include historic ore prospecting methods, local geology, insights into ore veins and stockworks, the local trend and distribution of ore channels, reverse faults, shattered rock above replacement ore bodies, mineral enrichment in oxidized and sulphide zones and more. **8.5″ X 11″, 66 ppgs, Retail Price: $8.99**

Mining in Colorado - Unavailable since 1926, this publication was originally compiled by the United States Department of Interior. This volume also includes important insights into the mining history of Colorado from its early beginnings in the 1850's right up to the mid 1920's. Not only is Colorado's gold mining heritage included, but also its silver, copper, lead and zinc mining industry. Each mining area is treated separately, detailing the development of Colorado's mines on a county by county basis. **8.5″ X 11″, 284 ppgs, Retail Price: $19.99**

Gold Mining in Gilpin County Colorado - Unavailable since 1876, this publication was originally compiled by the Register Steam Printing House of Central City, Colorado. A rare glimpse at the gold mining history and early mines of Gilpin County, Colorado from their first discovery in the 1850's up to the "flush years" of the mid 1870's. Of particular interest is the history of the discovery of gold in Gilpin County and details about the men who made those first strikes. Special focus is given to the early gold mines and first mining districts of the area, many of which are not detailed in other books on Colorado's gold mining history. **8.5″ X 11″, 156 ppgs, Retail Price: $12.99**

Mining in the Gold Brick Mining District of Colorado - Important insights into the history of the Gold Brick Mining District, as well as its local geography and economic geology. Also included are the histories and locations of historic mines in this important Colorado Mining District, including the Cortland, Carter, Raymond, Gold Links, Sacramento, Bassick, Sandy Hook, Chronicle, Grand Prize, Chloride, Granite Mountain, Lucille, Gray Mountain, Hilltop, Maggie Mitchell, Silver Islet, Revenue, Roosevelt, Carbonate King and others. In addition to hardrock mining, are also included are details on gold placer mining in this portion of Colorado. **8.5″ X 11″, 140 ppgs, Retail Price: $12.99**

Ore Deposits of the London Fault of Colorado - First published in 1941, it has been unavailable since those days and sheds important light on the mines and mineral deposits of the London Fault in Central Colorado's Alma Mining District. This publication sheds important light on the gold veins and lead-silver deposits of the Alma Mining District. Included are geologic details on the London Mine, American Mine, Havigorst Tunnel, Ophir Mine, Mosher Tunnel, London-Butte Mine, Venture Shaft, Hard-To-Beat Mine, Oliver Twist Tunnel, Sacramento Mine, Mudsill Mine, Sherwood Mine, Wagner, Barcoe Tunnel and other mines in this important mining region. 110 ppgs., 10.99

The Mines of Colorado - First published in 1867, it has been unavailable since those days and sheds important light on Colorado's early mining history. Written shortly after the events took place, this publication sheds important light on the Pike's Peak Gold Rush, the discovery of gold on Ralston Creek and Dry Creek in the 1850's, as well as details on the first wave of miners into Colorado and their trials and tribulations as they crossed the Great Plains. Also included are details on early discoveries of lode gold in the mountainous regions of Colorado, details on the early mines hardrock and placer mines, and much more. It is a veritable treasure trove on Colorado's early mining history and will be of great importance to anyone who is interested in the mining of gold or other minerals in Colorado, as well as those interested in the history of the state. 478 ppgs., 29.99

The La Plata Mining District of Colorado - Originally titled "Geology and Ore Deposits in the Vicinity of the La Plata District of Colorado" and first published in 1949, it has been unavailable since those days and sheds important light on the mines and mineral deposits of the La Plata Mining District of Colorado.214 ppgs., 19.99

The Carbonates of Leadville and the Formation of Coal in Colorado - First published in 1879, "Carbonates of Leadville: A Treatise on the Formation of Coal in Colorado" has been unavailable since those days and sheds important light on the history of the famous mining area in Colorado. Featured here are insights into the geology of Carbonates near Leadville, Colorado and the formation of coal deposits in that area. Also included are details on Assaying, Cupellation and Scorification methods used in mining. 112 ppgs., 11.99

The Catalpa Mining Company of Leadville, Colorado - This reprinted circular of the Catalpa Mining Company offers insight into one of the most important mines in the Leadville Mining District during the early 1880's - the famous Catalpa Mine. Also included are details on several adjoining mines in the area including the Evening Star, Pendery, Crescent, Carbonate, Yankee Doodle, Morning Star, Modoc, Etna and others. 70 ppgs., 8.99

The Summitville Mining District of the San Juan Mountains of Colorado - First published in 1960, "Geology and Ore Deposits of the Summitville Mining District San Juan Mountains of Colorado" has been unavailable since those days and sheds important light on the history of the famous mining area in Summit County, Colorado. Featured here in this fascinating text are insights into the local geology of this important Colorado Mining area. Lavishly illustrated with rare photos and hard to find mine maps. 104 ppgs., 10.99

Economic Geology of the Silverton Quadrangle of Colorado - First published in 1901, "Economic Geology of the Silverton Quadrangle Colorado" has been unavailable since those days and sheds important light on the history of the famous mining area in Colorado. Featured here in this fascinating text are insights into the local geology of this important Colorado Mining area, as well as into numerous mines. Lavishly illustrated with rare photos and hard to find mine maps. 304 ppgs., 24.99

Mining in Colorado in 1920 - First published in 1921, "The Annual Report for 1920" by the Colorado Bureau of Mines has been unavailable since those days and sheds important light on the history of the famous mining area in Colorado. Featured here are insights into the mineral industry of Colorado as it existed in 1920, complete with full statistics of all known operating gold, silver, copper and other mines that operated throughout the state. 90 ppgs., 9.99

Geology of the Glenwood Springs Quadrangle of North Western Colorado - First published in 1963, "Geology of the Glenwood Springs Quadrangle and Vicinity of North Western Colorado" has been unavailable since those days and sheds important light on the geology of this portion of North Western Colorado. Included are details on dozens of mines in this important mining Colorado region. 102 ppgs., 11.99

Men of Note Affiliated With Mining in the Cripple Creek Mining District - First published in 1905 by L.A. Snyder, "Men of note affiliated with mining and mining interests in the Cripple Creek district " has been unavailable since those days and sheds important light on the history of the famous Cripple Creek Mining District. Featured here in this fascinating text are insights into the movers and shakers who put the Cripple Creek Mining District on the map back in its heyday, including men like Bob Womack, Frank Campbell, James Wright, George Hill, J.E. Jones, Walter Swanson and dozens of others who discovered, owned and managed the leading mines of the Cripple Creek District. Also included are rare insights into the early mining history of this important mining district. Lavishly illustrated with rare photos from the early days of mining in Cripple Creek. 156 ppgs., 14.99

Ore Deposits Near Lake City, Colorado - First published in 1911, "Geology and Ore Deposits Near Lake City, Colorado" has been unavailable since those days and sheds important light on the geology and mining areas of this portion Colorado. Included are details on dozens of mines in this important mining Colorado region. 164 ppgs., 14.99

Ore Deposits of the Montezuma Quadrangle of Colorado - First published in 1935, "Ore Deposits of the Montezuma Quadrangle of Colorado" has been unavailable since those days and sheds important light on the history of the famous mining area in Summit County, Colorado. Featured here in this fascinating text are insights into the local geology, as well as dozens of important gold, silver and copper mines. Lavishly illustrated with rare photos and hard to find mine maps. 190 ppgs., 19.99

Ore Deposits of the Platoro and Summitville Mining Districts of Colorado - First published in 1917, "Ore Deposits of the Platoro and Summitville Mining Districts of Colorado" has been unavailable since those days and sheds important light on the history of the famous mining area in Summit County, Colorado. Featured here in this fascinating text are insights into the local geology, as well as dozens of mines in the Summitville, Platoro, Gilmore, Stunner and Jasper Mining Districts, including the Eurydice, Pass-Me-By, Asiatic, Watrous, Perry, Miser, Guadaloupe, Forest King, Parole, Morrimac, Congress, Mammoth, Golconda, Little Annie, Bobtail, Aztec and others. Lavishly illustrated with rare photos and hard to find mine maps. 184 ppgs., 19.99

Ore Deposits of the Creede Mining District of Colorado - First published in 1923, it has been unavailable since those days and sheds important light on the mines and mineral deposits of the Creede Mining District in Mineral County, Colorado. Included are geologic details on dozens of mines in this important mining Colorado region. 242 ppgs., 19.99

Ore Deposits of the Garfield Quadrangle of Colorado - First published in 1957, it has been unavailable since those days and sheds important light on the mines and mineral deposits of the Garfield Quadrangle in Garfield County, Colorado. Included are geologic details on dozens of mines in this important mining Colorado region. 144 ppgs., 12.99

<u>Ore Deposits of the Breckenridge Mining District of Colorado</u> - First published in 1911, it has been unavailable since those days and sheds important light on the mines and mineral deposits of the Breckenridge Mining District in Summit County, Colorado. Included are geologic details on dozens of mines in this important mining Colorado region.   246 ppgs., 19.99

<u>Ore Deposits of the Bonanza Mining District of Colorado</u> - First published in 1932, it has been unavailable since those days and sheds important light on the mines and mineral deposits of the Bonanza Mining District. Included are geologic details on dozens of mines in this important mining Colorado region.   232 ppgs., 24.99

East Coast Mining Books

<u>The Gold Fields of the Southern Appalachians</u> - Unavailable since 1895, this important publication was originally published by the US Department of Interior and has been unavailable for nearly 120 years. Topics include the geology, rock formations and the formation of ore deposits in this important mining area of the American South. Of particular focus is information on the history and statistics of the ore deposits in this area, their form and structure and veins. Also included are details on the placer gold deposits of the region. The gold fields of the Georgian Belt, Carolinian Belt and the South Mountain Mining District of North Carolina are all treated in descriptive detail. Included are hard to find details, including the descriptions and locations of numerous gold mines in Georgia, North Carolina and elsewhere in the American South. Also included are details on the gold belts of the British Maritime Provinces and the Green Mountains. **8.5" X 11", 104 ppgs, Retail Price: $9.99**

Gold Rush Tales Series

Millions in Siskiyou County Gold - In this first volume of the "Gold Rush Tales" series, leading mining historian and editor Kerby Jackson, introduces us to the story of how millions of dollars worth of gold was discovered in Siskiyou County during the California Gold Rush. Lavishly illustrated with photos from the 19th Century, this hard to find information was first published in 1897 and sheds important light onto the gold rush era in Siskiyou County, California and the experiences of the men who dug for the gold and actually found it. **8.5" X 11", 82 ppgs, Retail Price: $9.99**

The California Rand in the Days of '49 - In this second volume of the "Gold Rush Tales" series, leading mining historian and editor Kerby Jackson, introduces us to four tales from the California Gold Rush. Lavishly illustrated with photos from the 19th Century, this hard to find information was first published in 1890's and includes the stories of "California's Rand", details about Chinese miners, how one early miner named Baker struck it rich and also the story of Alphonzo Bowers, who invented the first hydraulic gold dredge. **8.5" X 11", 54 ppgs, Retail Price: $9.99**

Idaho Mining Books

Gold in Idaho - Unavailable since the 1940's, this publication was originally compiled by the Idaho Bureau of Mines and includes details on gold mining in Idaho. Included is not only raw data on gold production in Idaho, but also valuable insight into where gold may be found in Idaho, as well as practical information on the gold bearing rocks and other geological features that will assist those looking for placer and lode gold in the State of Idaho. This volume also includes thirteen gold maps that greatly enhance the practical usability of the information contained in this small book detailing where to find gold in Idaho. **8.5" X 11", 72 ppgs. Retail Price: $9.99**

Geology of the Couer D'Alene Mining District of Idaho - Unavailable since 1961, this publication was originally compiled by the Idaho Bureau of Mines and Geology and includes details on the mining of gold, silver and other minerals in the famous Coeur D'Alene Mining District in Northern Idaho. Included are details on the early history of the Coeur D'Alene Mining District, local tectonic settings, ore deposit features, information on the mineral belts of the Osburn Fault, as well as detailed information on the famous Bunker Hill Mine, the Dayrock Mine, Galena Mine, Lucky Friday Mine and the infamous Sunshine Mine. This volume also includes sixteen hard to find maps. **8.5" X 11", 70 ppgs. Retail Price: $9.99**

The Gold Camps and Silver Cities of Idaho - From 1963, this important publication on Idaho Mining has not been available for nearly fifty years. Included are rare insights into the history of Idaho's Gold Rush, as well as the mad craze for silver in the Idaho Panhandle. Documented in fine detail are the early mining excitements at Boise Basin, at South Boise, in the Owyhees, at Deadwood, Long Valley, Stanley Basin and Robinson Bar, at Atlanta, on the famous Boise River, Volcano, Little Smokey, Banner, Boise Ridge, Hailey, Leesburg, Lemhi, Pearl, at South Mountain, Shoup and Ulysses, Yellow Jacket and Loon Creek. The story follows with the appearance of Chinese miners at the new mining camps on the Snake River, Black Pine, Yankee Fork, Bay Horse, Clayton, Heath, Seven Devils, Gibbonsville, Vienna and Sawtooth City. Also included are special sections on the Idaho Lead and Silver mines of the late 1800's, as well as the mining discoveries of the early 1900's that paved the way for Idaho's modern mining and mineral industry. Lavishly illustrated with rare historic photos, this volume provides a one of a kind documentary into Idaho's mining history that is sure to be enjoyed by not only modern miners and prospectors who still scour the hills in search of nature's treasures, but also those enjoy history and tromping through overgrown ghost towns and long abandoned mining camps. **186 ppgs, $14.99**

Ore Deposits and Mining in North Western Custer County Idaho - Unavailable since 1913, this important publication was originally published by the Us Department of the Interior and has been unavailable for a century. Included are fine details on the geology, geography, gold placers and gold and silver bearing quartz veins of the mining region of North West Custer County, Idaho. Of particular interest is a rare look at the mines and prospects of the region, including those such as the Ramshorn Mine, SkyLark, Riverview, Excelsior, Beardsley, Pacific, Hoosier, Silver Brick, Forest Rose and dozens of others in the Bay Horse Mining District. Also covered are the mines of the Yankee Fork District such as the Lucky Boy, Badger, Black, Enterprise, Charles Dickens, Morrison, Golden Sunbeam, Montana, Golden Gate and others, as well as those in the Loon Mining District. **8.5" X 11", 126 ppgs. Retail Price: $12.99**

Gold Rush To Idaho - Unavailable since 1963, this important publication was originally published by the Idaho Bureau of Mines and has been unavailable for 50 years. "Gold Rush To Idaho" revisits the earliest years of the discovery of gold in Idaho Territory and introduces us to the conditions that the pioneer gold seekers met when they blazed a trail through the wilderness of Idaho's mountains and discovered the precious yellow metal at Oro Fino and Pierce. Subsequent rushes followed at places like Elk City, Newsome, Clearwater Station, Florence, Warrens and elsewhere. Of particular interest is a rare look at the hardships that the first miners in Idaho met with during their day to day existences and their attempts to bring law and order to their mining camps. **8.5" X 11", 88 ppgs. Retail Price: $9.99**

The Geology and Mines of Northern Idaho and North Western Montana - Unavailable since 1909, this important publication was originally published by the Us Department of the Interior and has been unavailable for a century. Included are fine details on the geology and geography of the mining regions of Northern Idaho and North Western Montana. Of particular interest is a rare look at the mines and prospects of the region, including those in the Pine Creek Mining District, Lake Pend Oreille district, Troy Mining District, Sylvanite District, Cabinet Mining District, Prospect Mining District and the Missoula Valley. Some of the mines featured include the Iron Mountain, Silver Butte, Snowshoe, Grouse Mountain Mine and others. **8.5" X 11", 142 ppgs. Retail Price: $12.99**

Mining in the Alturas Quadrangle of Blaine County Idaho - Unavailable since 1922, this important publication was originally published by the Idaho Bureau of Mines and has been unavailable for ninety years. Topics include the geology, rock formations and the formation of ore deposits in this important mining area of Idaho. Of particular focus is information on the local geology, quartz veins and ore deposits of this portion of Idaho. Included are hard to find details, including the descriptions and locations of numerous gold and silver mines in the area including the Silver King, Pilgrim, Columbia, Lone Jack, Sunbeam, Pride of the West, Lucky Boy, Scotia, Atlanta, Beaver-Bidwell and others mines and prospects. **8.5" X 11", 56 ppgs. Retail Price: $8.99**

Mining in Lemhi County Idaho - Originally published in 1913, this important book on Idaho Mining has not been available to miners for over a century. Included are rare insights into hundreds of gold, silver, copper and other mines in this famous Idaho mining area. Details include the locations, geology, history, production and other facts of the mines of this region, not only gold and silver hardrock mines, but also gold placer mines, lead-silver deposits, copper mines, cobalt-nickel deposits, tungsten and tin mines . It is lavishly illustrated with hard to find photos of the period and rare mining maps. Some of the vicinities featured include the Nicholia Mining District, Spring Mountain District, Texas District, Blue Wing District, Junction District, McDevitt District, Pratt Creek, Eldorado District, Kirtley Creek, Carmen Creek, Gibbonsville, Indian Creek, Mineral Hill District, Mackinaw, Eureka District, Blackbird District, YellowJacket District, Gravel Range District, Junction District, Parker Mountain and other mining districts. **8.5" X 11", 226 ppgs. Retail Price: $19.99**

Mining in Shoshone County Idaho - First published in 1923, it has been unavailable for over a century and sheds important light on the mining history of Shoshone County, Idaho. Some of the topics include the history of mining in Shoshone County, a look at the local geology and ore characteristics of lead-silver deposits, zinc deposits, copper, antimony, gold and other minerals. Also included are insights into the history, production, characteristics and locations of numerous mines in the area. 198 ppgs, 15.99

Geology of the Bitterroot and Clearwater Mountains of Idaho and Montana - Unavailable since 1904, this publication offers rare insights into the geology of this region of Idaho and Montana. Included are also details on the numerous gold, silver and copper mines of this region. 13.99, 150 ppgs

Gold in the Black Pine Mining District of Idaho - Unavailable since 1984, this publication offers rare insights into the famous Black Pine Mining District of Idaho. Included in this very small booklet are facts about the geology and ore deposits of this famous mining district in Idaho, as well as some insight into the early mining history of the district. 6.99, 44 pgs

Mining in Eastern Cassia County Idaho - Unavailable since 1931, this publication offers rare insights into this famous mining region of Idaho. Included are descriptions of numerous gold and silver mines, their locations, how they were established and how they operated, as well as their geologic structures. 19.99, 226 ppgs

<u>Geology of the Alder Creek Mining District of Idaho</u> - Unavailable since 1968, this publication offers rare insights into the famous Alder Creek Mining District of Idaho. Included in this small booklet are facts about the geology and ore deposits of this famous mining district in Idaho. 7.99, 58 ppgs

<u>Mines of the Alder Creek Mining District of Idaho</u> - Unavailable since 1997, this publication offers rare insights into the famous Alder Creek Mining District of Idaho. Included in this small booklet are facts about Empire Mine, Blue Bird or Easlie Mine, Champion Mine, Doughboy Mine, Horseshoe Mine and White Knob Group. Included are descriptions of each mine, their locations, how they were established and how they operated. Lavishly illustrated with hard to find mine maps and rare historical photographs. 8.99, 80 ppgs

Montana Mining Books

<u>A History of Butte Montana: The World's Greatest Mining Camp</u> - First published in 1900 by H.C. Freeman, this important publication sheds a bright light on one of the most important mining areas in the history of The West. Together with his insights, as well as rare photographs of the periods, Harry Freeman describes Butte and its vicinity from its early beginnings, right up to its flush years when copper flowed from its mines like a river. At the time of publication, Butte, Montana was known worldwide as "The Richest Mining Spot On Earth" and produced not only vast amounts of copper, but also silver, gold and other metals from its mines. Freeman illustrates, with great detail, the most important mines in the vicinity of Butte, providing rare details on their owners, their history and most importantly, how the mines operated and how their treasures were extracted. Of particular interest are the dozens of rare photographs that depict mines such as the famous Anaconda, the Silver Bow, the Smoke House, Moose, Paulin, Buffalo, Little Minah, the Mountain Consolidated, West Greyrock, Cora, the Green Mountain, Diamond, Bell, Parnell, the Neversweat, Nipper, Original and many others. **8.5" X 11", 142 ppgs. Retail Price: $12.99**

<u>The Butte Mining District of Montana</u> - This important publication on Montana Mining has not been available for over a century. Included are rare insights into the gold, copper and silver mines of Butte, Montana together with hard to find maps and photographs. Some of the topics include the early history of gold, silver and copper mining in the Butte area, insight into the geology of its mining areas, the local distribution of gold, silver and copper ores, as well their composition and how to identify them. Also included are detailed facts about the mines in the Butte Mining District, including the famous Anaconda Mine, Gagnon, Parrot, Blue Vein, Moscow, Poulin, Stella, Buffalo, Green Mountain, Wake Up Jim, the Diamond-Bell Group, Mountain Consolidated, East Greyrock, West Greyrock, Snowball, Corra, Speculator, Adirondack, Miners Union, the Jessie-Edith May Group, Otisco, Iduna, Colorado, Lizzie, Cambers, Anderson, Hesperus, Preferencia and dozens of others. **8.5" X 11", 298 ppgs. Retail Price: $24.99**

<u>Mines of the Helena Mining Region of Montana</u> - This important publication on Montana Mining has not been available for over a century. Included are rare insights into the gold, copper and silver mines of the vicinity of Helena, Montana, including the Marysville Mining District, Elliston Mining District, Rimini Mining District, Helena Mining District, Clancy Mining District, Wickes Mining District, Boulder and Basin Mining Districts and the Elkhorn Mining District. Some of the topics include the early history of gold, silver and copper mining in the Helena area, insight into the geology of its mining areas, the local distribution of gold, silver and copper ores, as well their composition and how to identify them. Also included are detailed facts, history, geology and locations of over one hundred gold, silver and copper mines in the area . **8.5" X 11", 162 ppgs, Retail Price: $14.99**

<u>Mines and Geology of the Garnet Range of Montana</u> - This important publication on Montana Mining has not been available for over a century. Included are rare insights into the gold, copper and silver mines of the vicinity of this important mining area of Montana. Some of the topics include the early history of gold, silver and copper mining in the Garnet Mountains, insight into the geology of its mining areas, the local distribution of gold, silver and copper ores, as well their composition and how to identify them. Also included are detailed facts, history, geology and locations of numerous gold, silver and copper mines in the area . **8.5" X 11", 100 ppgs, Retail Price: $11.99**

<u>Mines and Geology of the Philipsburg Quadrangle of Montana</u> - This important publication on Montana Mining has not been available for over a century. Included are rare insights into the gold, copper and silver mines of the vicinity of this important mining area of Montana. Some of the topics include the early history of gold, silver and copper mining in the Philipsburg Quadrangle, insight into the geology of its mining areas, the local distribution of gold, silver and copper ores, as well their composition and how to identify them. Also included are detailed facts, history, geology and locations of over one hundred gold, silver and copper mines in the area **8.5" X 11", 290 ppgs, Retail Price: $24.99**

<u>Geology of the Marysville Mining District of Montana</u> - Included are rare insights into the mining geology of the Marysville Mining District. Some of the topics include the early history of gold, silver and copper mining in the area, insight into the geology of its mining areas, the local distribution of gold, silver and copper ores, as well their composition and how to identify them. Also included are detailed facts, history, geology and locations of gold, silver and copper mines in the area **8.5" X 11", 198 ppgs, Retail Price: $19.99**

The Geology and Mines of Northern Idaho and North Western Montana- See listing under Idaho.

The History of Gold Dredging in Montana - Unavailable since 1916, this important publication was originally published by the Us Bureau of Mines and has been unavailable for a century. A century and more ago, giant dredging machines dug in Montana's rivers and creeks in search of illusive golden riches. First appearing in California in the 1850's, gold dredges finally reached their peak of development in Siberia and New Zealand before becoming popular again in the United States. This book offers a unique historical perspective on the gold dredges that once operated in Montana. This book on Montana mining history is lavishly illustrated with dozens of rare historic photos gold dredges that once operated in Montana, as well as hard to locate plans on how these dredges were designed. 120 ppgs., 11.99

The Great Dynamite Explosion at Butte, Montana - On the night of January 15th, 1895, the great mining center of Butte, Montana was devastated by a series of explosions. As the Reno Daily Journal's headline blared: DYNAMITE EXPLOSION. Terrible Loss of Life at Butte, Montana. ABOUT 150 KILLED AND INJURED. The Fire Department Annihilated-Windows Demolished a Mile Away. The Daily Journal continued, "A fire broke out in the Butte Hardware Company's warehouse near Butte City, Montana. There was a large quantity of giant powder stored in the building and when the Fire Department was fighting the flames the powder exploded killing every fireman except two. While the dead and wounded were being removed another explosion occurred which killed more persons, including several policemen and citizens. Many persons were torn to fragments and others were shocked to death by the concussion. Later a third explosion occurred increasing the number of deaths and adding to the ruin and devastation." Almost as soon as the fires had cooled, local educator John F. Davies set pen to paper to record for history what took place, including the accounts of some of those who saw history unfold first hand. 74 ppgs., 9.99

Nevada Mining Books

The Bull Frog Mining District of Nevada - Unavailable since 1910, this publication was originally compiled by the United States Department of Interior. This volume also includes important insights into the geologic formations, faults and other aspects of economic geology in this Nevada mining district. Of particular interest are the fine details on many mines in the area, including their locations, histories, development and mineralization. Some of the mines featured include the National Bank Mine, Providence, Gibraltor, Tramps, Denver, Original Bullfrog, Gold Bar, Mayflower, Homestake-King and other mines and prospects. **8.5" X 11", 152 ppgs, Retail Price: $14.99**

History of the Comstock Lode - Unavailable since 1876, this publication was originally released by John Wiley & Sons. This volume also includes important insights into the famous Comstock Lode of Nevada that represented the first major silver discovery in the United States. During its spectacular run, the Comstock produced over 192 million ounces of silver and 8.2 million ounces of gold. Not only did the Comstock result in one of the largest mining rushes in history and yield immense fortunes for its owners, but it made important contributions to the development of the State of Nevada, as well as neighboring California. Included here are important details on not only the early development and history of the Comstock, but also rare early insight into its mines, ore and its geology.**8.5" X 11", 244 ppgs, Retail Price: $19.99**

The Pioche Mining District of Nevada - First published in 1932, it has been unavailable for over a century and sheds important light on the mining history of Nevada. Some of the topics include the history of mining in this district, as well as the characteristics of its mineral and ore deposits. Also included are insights into the history, production, characteristics and locations of numerous mines in the area. Some of the mines include the Combined Metals, Pioche, Ely Valley, No. 10, Poorman, Wide Awake, Alps, Prince, Virginia Louise, Half Moon, Abe Lincoln, Fairview, Bristol Silver, National, Vesuvius, Inman, Tempest, Hillside, Jackrabbit, Lucky Star, Fortuna, Mendha, Manhattan, Hamburg, Comet, Lyndon and others. 108 ppgs 10.99

The Yerington Mining District of Nevada - First published in 1932, it has been unavailable for over a century and sheds important light on the mining history of Nevada. Some of the topics include the history of mining in this district, as well as the characteristics of its mineral and ore deposits. Also included are insights into the history, production, characteristics and locations of numerous mines in the area. Some of the mines include the Bluestone, Mason Valley, Malachite, McConnell, Greenwood, Western Nevada, Ludwig, Douglas Hill, Casting Copper, Montana-Yerington, Empire, Jim Beatty, Terry and McFarland, Blue Jay and others. 92 ppgs, 10.99

The Genesis of the Ores of Tonopah Nevada - Unavailable since 1918, this hard to find publication includes valuable insights into the gold mines around Tonopah, Nevada. The publication includes important details into the geology of mines in the Tonopah Mining District of Nevada. 90 ppgs, 10.99

Mining Camps of Elko, Lander and Eureka Counties Nevada - Unavailable since 1910, this hard to find publication includes valuable insights into the mining camps of Elko, Lander and Eureka Counties, Nevada. The publication includes important details into the history of mines and mining in these three Nevada counties. 154 ppgs, 12.99

<u>Ore Deposits of the Bullfrog Quadrangle</u> - Unavailable since 1964 and released as "Geology of Bullfrog Quadrangle and Ore Deposits Related to Bullfrog Hills Caldera, Nye County, Nevada and Inyo County, California". The publication includes important details into the geology of mines in the Bullfrog Quadrangle of Nye County, Nevada and Inyo County, California. 52 ppgs, 9.99

<u>Mining in Eureka County Nevada</u> - Unavailable since 1879, this hard to find publication includes valuable insights into the early mining history off Eureka County, Nevada. The publication includes important details into the early history of the mines of Eureka County, as well as their development, production and how their ores were treated. Also included are details on the 1872 Mining Act, as well as the local rules, regulations and customs of the miners in Eureka County.134 ppgs, 12.99

New Mexico Mining Books

<u>The Mogollon Mining District of New Mexico</u> - Unavailable since 1927, this important publication was originally published by the US Department of Interior and has been unavailable for 80 years. Topics include the geology, rock formations and the formation of ore deposits in this important mining area in New Mexico. Of particular focus is information on the history and production of the ore deposits in this area, their form and structure, vein filling, their paragenesis, origins and ore shoots, as well as oxidation and supergene enrichment. Also included are hard to find details, including the descriptions and locations of numerous gold, silver and other types of mines, including the Eureka, Pacific, South Alpine, Great Western, Enterprise, Buffalo, Mountain View, Floride, Gold Dust, Last Chance, Deadwood, Confidence, Maud S., Deep Down, Little Fanney, Trilby, Johnson, Alberta, Comet, Golden Eagle, Cooney, Queen, the Iron Crown, Eberle, Clifton, Andrew Jackson mine, Mascot and others. **8.5" X 11", 144 ppgs, Retail Price: $12.99**

<u>The Percha Mining District of Kingston New Mexico</u> - Unavailable since 1883, this important publication was originally published by the Kingston Tribune and has been unavailable for over one hundred and thirty five years. Having been written during the earliest years of gold and silver mining in the Percha Mining District, unlike other books on the subject, this work offers the unique perspective of having actually been written while the early mining history of this area was still being made. In fact, the work was written so early in the development of this area that many of the notable mines in the Percha District were less than a few years old and were still being operated by their original discoverers with the same enthusiasm as when they were first located. Included are hard to find details on the very earliest gold and silver mines of this important mining district near Kingston in Sierra County, New Mexico. **8.5" X 11", 68 ppgs, Retail Price: $9.99**

<u>Economic Geology of New Mexico</u> - Written in 1908, this hard to find publication includes valuable insights into the mining industry of New Mexico. Included are important details on the economic geology of New Mexico, including the general locations of numerous valuable minerals in New Mexico **8.5" X 11", 76 ppgs, Retail Price: $8.99**

<u>The Magdalena Mining District of New Mexico</u> - Written in 1942, this hard to find publication includes valuable insights into the gold and silver mining industry of New Mexico. Included are important details on the geology and ore minerals of the Magdalena Mining District, as well as the locations and other facts of the important gold and silver mines of the area. Some of the mines featured include the Nitt, Graphic-Waldo or Ozark Mine, Kelly Mine, Juanita, South Juanita, Black Cloud, Mistletoe, Young America, Imperial, Enterprise, Linchburg Tunnel, Woodland, Cavern, Grand Ledge, Connelly, West Virginia, Victor, Sampson, Grand Tower, Legal Tender, Germany, Little Loella, Tip Top, Key, Stonewall, Ambrosia, Sleeper, Hardscrabble, Anchor, Vindicator, Cavalier, Heister and others. Lavishly illustrated with photographs of local ore, mine maps and more. **8.5" X 11", 230 ppgs, Retail Price: $19.99**

<u>Mineral Belts of Western Sierra County New Mexico</u> - Written in 1979, this hard to find publication includes valuable insights into the mining industry of New Mexico. Included are important details on the gold and silver bearing mineral belts of Western Sierra County, New Mexico. **8.5" X 11", 80 ppgs, Retail Price: $8.99**

Oregon Mining Books

<u>Geology and Mineral Resources of Josephine County, Oregon</u> - Unavailable since the 1970's, this important publication was originally compiled by the Oregon Department of Geology and Mineral Industries and includes important details on the economic geology and mineral resources of this important mining area in South Western Oregon. Included are notes on the history, geology and development of important mines, as well as insights into the mining of gold, copper, nickel, limestone, chromium and other minerals found in large quantities in Josephine County, Oregon. **8.5" X 11", 54 ppgs. Retail Price: $9.99**

Mines and Prospects of the Mount Reuben Mining District - Unavailable since 1947, this important publication was originally compiled by geologist Elton Youngberg of the Oregon Department of Geology and Mineral Industries and includes detailed descriptions, histories and the geology of the Mount Reuben Mining District in Josephine County, Oregon. Included are notes on the history, geology, development and assay statistics, as well as underground maps of all the major mines and prospects in the vicinity of this much neglected mining district. **8.5" X 11", 48 ppgs. Retail Price: $9.99**

The Granite Mining District - Notes on the history, geology and development of important mines in the well known Granite Mining District which is located in Grant County, Oregon. Some of the mines discussed include the Ajax, Blue Ribbon, Buffalo, Continental, Cougar-Independence, Magnolia, New York, Standard and the Tillicum. Also included are many rare maps pertaining to the mines in the area. **8.5" X 11", 48 ppgs. Retail Price: $9.99**

Ore Deposits of the Takilma and Waldo Mining Districts of Josephine County, Oregon - The Waldo and Takilma mining districts are most notable for the fact that the earliest large scale mining of placer gold and copper in Oregon took place in these two areas. Included are details about some of the earliest large gold mines in the state such as the Llano de Oro, High Gravel, Cameron, Platerica, Deep Gravel and others, as well as copper mines such as the famous Queen of Bronze mine, the Waldo, Lily and Cowboy mines. This volume also includes six maps and 20 original illustrations. **8.5" X 11", 74 ppgs. Retail Price: $9.99**

Metal Mines of Douglas, Coos and Curry Counties, Oregon - Oregon mining historian Kerby Jackson introduces us to a classic work on Oregon's mining history in this important re-issue of Bulletin 14C Volume 1, otherwise known as the Douglas, Coos & Curry Counties, Oregon Metal Mines Handbook. Unavailable since 1940, this important publication was originally compiled by the Oregon Department of Geology and Mineral Industries includes detailed descriptions, histories and the geology of over 250 metallic mineral mines and prospects in this rugged area of South West Oregon. **8.5" X 11", 158 ppgs. Retail Price: $19.99**

Metal Mines of Jackson County, Oregon - Unavailable since 1943, this important publication was originally compiled by the Oregon Department of Geology and Mineral Industries includes detailed descriptions, histories and the geology of over 450 metallic mineral mines and prospects in Jackson County, Oregon. Included are such famous gold mining areas as Gold Hill, Jacksonville, Sterling and the Upper Applegate. **8.5" X 11", 220 ppgs. Retail Price: $24.99**

Metal Mines of Josephine County, Oregon - Oregon mining historian Kerby Jackson introduces us to a classic work on Oregon's mining history in this important re-issue of Bulletin 14C, otherwise known as the Josephine County, Oregon Metal Mines Handbook. Unavailable since 1952, this important publication was originally compiled by the Oregon Department of Geology and Mineral Industries includes detailed descriptions, histories and the geology of over 500 metallic mineral mines and prospects in Josephine County, Oregon. **8.5" X 11", 250 ppgs. Retail Price: $24.99**

Metal Mines of North East Oregon - Oregon mining historian Kerby Jackson introduces us to a classic work on Oregon's mining history in this important re-issue of Bulletin 14A and 14B, otherwise known as the North East Oregon Metal Mines Handbook. Unavailable since 1941, this important publication was originally compiled by the Oregon Department of Geology and Mineral Industries and includes detailed descriptions, histories and the geology of over 750 metallic mineral mines and prospects in North Eastern Oregon. **8.5" X 11", 310 ppgs. Retail Price: $29.99**

Metal Mines of North West Oregon - Oregon mining historian Kerby Jackson introduces us to a classic work on Oregon's mining history in this important re-issue of Bulletin 14D, otherwise known as the North West Oregon Metal Mines Handbook. Unavailable since 1951, this important publication was originally compiled by the Oregon Department of Geology and Mineral Industries and includes detailed descriptions, histories and the geology of over 250 metallic mineral mines and prospects in North Western Oregon. **8.5" X 11", 182 ppgs. Retail Price: $19.99**

Mines and Prospects of Oregon - Mining historian Kerby Jackson introduces us to a classic mining work by the Oregon Bureau of Mines in this important re-issue of The Handbook of Mines and Prospects of Oregon. Unavailable since 1916, this publication includes important insights into hundreds of gold, silver, copper, coal, limestone and other mines that operated in the State of Oregon around the turn of the 19th Century. Included are not only geological details on early mines throughout Oregon, but also insights into their history, production, locations and in some cases, also included are rare maps of their underground workings. **8.5" X 11", 314 ppgs. Retail Price: $24.99**

Lode Gold of the Klamath Mountains of Northern California and South West Oregon
(See California Mining Books)

Mineral Resources of South West Oregon - Unavailable since 1914, this publication includes important insights into dozens of mines that once operated in South West Oregon, including the famous gold fields of Josephine and Jackson Counties, as well as the Coal Mines of Coos County. Included are not only geological details on early mines throughout South West Oregon, but also insights into their history, production and locations. **8.5" X 11", 154 ppgs. Retail Price: $11.99**

Chromite Mining in The Klamath Mountains of California and Oregon
(See California Mining Books)

Southern Oregon Mineral Wealth - Unavailable since 1904, this rare publication provides a unique snapshot into the mines that were operating in the area at the time. Included are not only geological details on early mines throughout South West Oregon, but also insights into their history, production and locations. Some of the mining areas include Grave Creek, Greenback, Wolf Creek, Jump Off Joe Creek, Granite Hill, Galice, Mount Reuben, Gold Hill, Galls Creek, Kane Creek, Sardine Creek, Birdseye Creek, Evans Creek, Foots Creek, Jacksonville, Ashland, the Applegate River, Waldo, Kerby and the Illinois River, Althouse and Sucker Creek, as well as insights into local copper mining and other topics. **8.5" X 11", 64 ppgs. Retail Price: $8.99**

Geology and Ore Deposits of the Takilma and Waldo Mining Districts - Unavailable since the 1933, this publication was originally compiled by the United States Geological Survey and includes details on gold and copper mining in the Takilma and Waldo Districts of Josephine County, Oregon. The Waldo and Takilma mining districts are most notable for the fact that the earliest large scale mining of placer gold and copper in Oregon took place in these two areas. Included in this report are details about some of the earliest large gold mines in the state such as the Llano de Oro, High Gravel, Cameron, Platerica, Deep Gravel and others, as well as copper mines such as the famous Queen of Bronze mine, the Waldo, Lily and Cowboy mines. In addition to geological examinations, insights are also provided into the production, day to day operations and early histories of these mines, as well as calculations of known mineral reserves in the area. This volume also includes six maps and 20 original illustrations. **8.5" X 11", 74 ppgs. Retail Price: $9.99**

Gold Mines of Oregon - Oregon mining historian Kerby Jackson introduces us to a classic work on Oregon's mining history in this important re-issue of Bulletin 61, otherwise known as "Gold and Silver In Oregon". Unavailable since 1968, this important publication was originally compiled by geologists Howard C. Brooks and Len Ramp of the Oregon Department of Geology and Mineral Industries and includes detailed descriptions, histories and the geology of over 450 gold mines Oregon. Included are notes on the history, geology and gold production statistics of all the major mining areas in Oregon including the Klamath Mountains, the Blue Mountains and the North Cascades. While gold is where you find it, as every miner knows, the path to success is to prospect for gold where it was previously found. **8.5" X 11", 344 ppgs. Retail Price: $24.99**

Mines and Mineral Resources of Curry County Oregon - Originally published in 1916, this important publication on Oregon Mining has not been available for nearly a century. Included are rare insights into the history, production and locations of dozens of gold mines in Curry County, Oregon, as well as detailed information on important Oregon mining districts in that area such as those at Agness, Bald Face Creek, Mule Creek, Boulder Creek, China Diggings, Collier Creek, Elk River, Gold Beach, Rock Creek, Sixes River and elsewhere. Particular attention is especially paid to the famous beach gold deposits of this portion of the Oregon Coast. **8.5" X 11", 140 ppgs. Retail Price: $11.99**

Chromite Mining in South West Oregon - Originally published in 1961, this important publication on Oregon Mining has not been available for nearly a century. Included are rare insights into the history, production and locations of nearly 300 chromite mines in South Western Oregon. **8.5" X 11", 184 ppgs. Retail Price: $14.99**

Mineral Resources of Douglas County Oregon - Originally published in 1972, this important publication on Oregon Mining has not been available for nearly forty years. Included are rare insights into the geology, history, production and locations of numerous gold mines and other mining properties in Douglas County, Oregon. **8.5" X 11", 124 ppgs. Retail Price: $11.99**

Mineral Resources of Coos County Oregon - Originally published in 1972, this important publication on Oregon Mining has not been available for nearly forty years. Included are rare insights into the geology, history, production and locations of numerous gold mines and other mining properties in Coos County, Oregon. **8.5" X 11", 100 ppgs. Retail Price: $11.99**

Mineral Resources of Lane County Oregon - Originally published in 1938, this important publication on Oregon Mining has not been available for nearly seventy five years. Included are extremely rare insights into the geology and mines of Lane County, Oregon, in particular in the Bohemia, Blue River, Oakridge, Black Butte and Winberry Mining Districts. **8.5" X 11", 82 ppgs. Retail Price: $9.99**

Mineral Resources of the Upper Chetco River of Oregon: Including the Kalmiopsis Wilderness - Originally published in 1975, this important publication on Oregon Mining has not been available for nearly forty years. Withdrawn under the 1872 Mining Act since 1984, real insight into the minerals resources and mines of the Upper Chetco River has long been unavailable due to the remoteness of the area. Despite this, the decades of battle between property owners and environmental extremists over the last private mining inholding in the area has continued to pique the interest of those interested in mining and other forms of natural resource use. Gold mining began in the area in the 1850's and has a rich history in this geographic area, even if the facts surrounding it are little known. Included are twenty two rare photographs, as well as insights into the Becca and Morning Mine, the Emmly Mine (also known as Emily Camp), the Frazier Mine, the Golden Dream or Higgins Mine, Hustis Mine, Peck Mine and others. **8.5" X 11", 64 ppgs. Retail Price: $8.99**

Gold Dredging in Oregon - Originally published in 1939, this important publication on Oregon Mining has not been available for nearly seventy five years. Included are extremely rare insights into the history and day to day operations of the dragline and bucketline gold dredges that once worked the placer gold fields of South West and North East Oregon in decades gone by. Also included are details into the areas that were worked by gold dredges in Josephine, Jackson, Baker and Grant counties, as well as the economic factors that impacted this mining method. This volume also offers a unique look into the values of river bottom land in relation to both farming and mining, in how farm lands were mined, re-soiled and reclamated after the dredges worked them. Featured are hard to find maps of the gold dredge fields, as well as rare photographs from a bygone era. **8.5" X 11", 86 ppgs. Retail Price: $8.99**

Quick Silver Mining in Oregon - Originally published in 1963, this important publication on Oregon Mining has not been available for over fifty years. This publication includes details into the history and production of Elemental Mercury or Quicksilver in the State of Oregon.   **8.5" X 11", 238 ppgs. Retail Price: $15.99**

Mines of the Greenhorn Mining District of Grant County Oregon - Originally published in 1948, this important publication on Oregon Mining has not been available for over sixty five years. In this publication are rare insights into the mines of the famous Greenhorn Mining District of Grant County, Oregon, especially the famous Morning Mine. Also included are details on the Tempest, Tiger, Bi-Metallic, Windsor, Psyche, Big Johnny, Snow Creek, Banzette and Paramount Mines, as well as prospects in the vicinities in the famous mining areas of Mormon Basin, Vinegar Basin and Desolation Creek. Included are hard to find mine maps and dozens of rare photographs from the bygone era of Grant County's rich mining history. **8.5" X 11", 72 ppgs. Retail Price: $9.99**

Geology of the Wallowa Mountains of Oregon: Part I (Volume 1) - Originally published in 1938, this important publication on Oregon Mining has not been available for nearly seventy five years. Included are details on the geology of this unique portion of North Eastern Oregon. This is the first part of a two book series on the area. Accompanying the text are rare photographs and historic maps. **8.5" X 11", 92 ppgs. Retail Price: $9.99**

Geology of the Wallowa Mountains of Oregon: Part II (Volume 2) - Originally published in 1938, this important publication on Oregon Mining has not been available for nearly seventy five years. Included are details on the geology of this unique portion of North Eastern Oregon. This is the first part of a two book series on the area. Accompanying the text are rare photographs and historic maps. **8.5" X 11", 94 ppgs. Retail Price: $9.99**

Field Identification of Minerals For Oregon Prospectors - Originally published in 1940, this important publication on Oregon Mining has not been available for nearly seventy five years. Included in this volume is an easy system for testing and identifying a wide range of minerals that might be found by prospectors, geologists and rockhounds in the State of Oregon, as well as in other locales. Topics include how to put together your own field testing kit and how to conduct rudimentary tests in the field. This volume is written in a clear and concise way to make it useful even for beginners. **8.5" X 11", 158 ppgs. Retail Price: $14.99**

The Bohemia Mining District of Oregon - Originally published in 1900, this important publication on Oregon Mining has not been available for over a century. Included in this volume are important insights into the famous Bohemia Mining District of Oregon, including the histories and locations of important gold mines in the area such as the Ophir Mine, Clarence, Acturas, Peek-a-boo, White Swan, Combination Mine, the Musick Mine, The California, White Ghost, The Mystery, Wall Street, Vesuvius, Story, Lizzie Bullock, Delta, Elsie Dora, Golden Slipper, Broadway, Champion Mine, Knott, Noonday, Helena, White Wings, Riverside and others. Also included are notes on the nearby Blue River Mining District. **8.5" X 11", 58 ppgs. Retail Price: $9.99**

The Gold Fields of Eastern Oregon - Unavailable since 1900, this publication was originally compiled by the Baker City Chamber of Commerce Offering important insights into the gold mining history of Eastern Oregon, "The Gold Fields of Eastern Oregon" sheds a rare light on many of the gold mines that were operating at the turn of the 19th Century in Baker County and Grant County in North Eastern Oregon. Some of the areas featured include the Cable Cove District, Baisely-Elhorn, Granite, Red Boy, Bonanza, Susanville, Sparta, Virtue, Vaughn, Sumpter, Burnt River, Rye Valley and other mining districts. Included is basic information on not only many gold mines that are well known to those interested in Eastern Oregon mining history, but also many mines and prospects which have been mostly lost to the passage of time. Accompanying are numerous rare photos **8.5" X 11", 78 ppgs. Retail Price: $10.99**

Gold Mining in Eastern Oregon - Originally published in 1938, this important publication on Oregon Mining has not been available for over a century. Included in this volume are important insights into the famous mining districts of Eastern Oregon during the late 1930's. Particular attention is given to those gold mines with milling and concentrating facilities in the Greenhorn, Red Boy, Alamo, Bonanza, Granite, Cable Cove, Cracker Creek, Virtue, Keating, Medical Springs, Sanger, Sparta, Chicken Creek, Mormon Basin, Connor Creek, Cornucopia and the Bull Run Mining Districts. Some of the mines featured include the Ben Harrison, North Pole-Columbia, Highland Maxwell, Baisley-Elkhorn, White Swan, Balm Creek, Twin Baby, Gem of Sparta, New Deal, Gleason, Gifford-Johnson, Cornucopia, Record, Bull Run, Orion and others. Of particular interest are the mill flow sheets and descriptions of milling operations of these mines. **8.5" X 11", 68 ppgs. Retail Price: $8.99**

The Gold Belt of the Blue Mountains of Oregon - Originally published in 1901, this important publication on Oregon Mining has not been available for over a century. Included in this volume are rare insights into the gold deposits of the Blue Mountains of North East Oregon, including the history of their early discovery and early production. Extensive details are offered on this important mining area's mineralogy and economic geology, as well as insights into nearby gold placers, silver deposits and copper deposits. Featured are the Elkhorn and Rock Creek mining districts, the Pocahontas district, Auburn and Minersville districts, Sumpter and Cracker Creek, Cable Cove, the Camp Carson district, Granite, Alamo, Greenhorn, Robinsonville, the Upper Burnt River Valley and Bonanza districts, Susanville, Quartzburg, Canyon Creek, Virtue, the Copper Butte district, the North Powder River, Sparta, Eagle Creek, Cornucopia, Pine Creek, Lower Powder River, the Upper Snake River Canyon, Rye Valley, Lower Burnt River Valley, Mormon Basin, the Malheur and Clarks Creek districts, Sutton Creek and others. Of particular interest are important details on numerous gold mines and prospects in these mining districts, including their locations, histories, geology and other important information, as well as information on silver, copper and fire opal deposits. **8.5″ X 11″, 250 ppgs. Retail Price: $24.99**

Mining in the Cascades Range of Oregon - Originally published in 1938, this important publication on Oregon Mining has not been available for over seventy five years. Included in this volume are rare insights into the gold mines and other types of metal mines in the Cascades Mountain Range of Oregon. Some of the important mining areas covered include the famous Bohemia Mining District, the North Santiam Mining District, Quartzville Mining District, Blue River Mining District, Fall Creek Mining District, Oakridge District, Zinc District, Buzzard-Al Sarena District, Grand Cove, Climax District and Barron Mining District. Of particular interest are important details on over 100 mines and prospects in these mining districts, including their locations, histories, geology and other important information. **8.5″ X 11″, 170 ppgs. Retail Price: $14.99**

Beach Gold Placers of the Oregon Coast - Originally published in 1934, this important publication on Oregon Mining has not been available for over 80 years. Included in this volume are rare insights into the beach gold deposits of the State of Oregon, including their locations, occurance, composition and geology. Of particular interest is information on placer platinum in Oregon's rich beach deposits. Also included are the locations and other information on some famous Oregon beach mines, including the Pioneer, Eagle, Chickamin, Iowa and beach placer mines north of the mouth of the Rogue River. **8.5″ X 11″, 60 ppgs. Retail Price: $8.99**

Mineralogical Composition of the Sands of the Oregon Coast: From Coos Bay to the Columbia – Published in 1945, he text features hard to find information on the composition of the gold bearing black sands of the South West Oregon Coast, offering a unique insight to prospectors in search of Oregon's legendary beach gold. 104 ppgs, $9.99

Manganese Mining in Oregon - First released in 1942 and now out of print, this special reprint edition of "Manganese in Oregon" was originally published by the Oregon Department of Geology and Mineral Industries. The text features hard to find information on the mining of Manganese in Oregon, including details and maps of Oregon manganese mines and prospects. 108 ppgs, 9.99

Medford Oregon As A Mining Center - Written in 1912, this hard to find publication includes valuable insights into the mining history of South West Oregon. This small book contains interesting information on the gold, copper and mining industry in Southern Oregon as it existed just prior to World War One, shedding light on some of the important mines in the area. Included are rare photographs and vintage advertising of the day. 80 ppgs, 9.99

Mineral Resources of Curry County Oregon - First released in 1977 and now out of print, this special reprint edition of "Geology, Mineral Resources and Rock Materials of Curry County, Oregon" was originally published in cooperation of Curry County, Oregon and the Oregon Department of Geology and Mineral Industries. The text features hard to find information on not only the mining of gold and other metals in Curry County, but also aggregate mining in the area. 102 ppgs, 11.99

Origin of the Gold Bearing Black Sands of the Coast of South West Oregon - First released in 1943 and now out of print, this special reprint edition of "The Origin of the Black Sands of the South West Oregon Coast" was originally published by the Oregon Department of Geology and Mineral Industries. The text features hard to find information on the origin of the gold bearing black sands of the South West Oregon Coast, offering a unique insight to prospectors in search of Oregon's legendary beach gold. 52 ppgs, 8.99

South West Oregon Mining - Leading mining historian Kerby Jackson introduces us to six classic small mining publications on the Gold Mining Industry in Southern Oregon. This small book consists of a compilation of USGS J.S. Diller's "Mines of the Riddles Quadrangle", "The Rogue River Valley Coal Fields" and "Mineral Resources of the Grants Pass Quadrangle", the Grants Pass Commercial Club's rare publication "Mining in Josephine County, Oregon" and the USGS publication "The Distribution of Placer Gold in the Sixes River, South West Oregon". Also included is F.W. Libbey's legendary article on the Southern Oregon Mining Industry, "Lest We Forget", which appeared in the publication of the Oregon State Department of Geology and Mineral Industries in the early 1960's. This compilation offers a unique perspective on mining in South West Oregon and includes considerable information on mines in Josephine, Jackson and Coos Counties. 142 ppgs, 14.99

<u>Geology and Mineral Resources of the Gasquet Quadrangle of California-Oregon</u> - First published in 1953, it has been unavailable for over a century and sheds important light on the geological features and mineral resources of this portion of Northern California and Southern Oregon. 80 ppgs, 9.99

<u>The Little North Santiam Mining District of Oregon</u> - Unavailable since 1985, this publication offers rare insights into one of the most famous mining areas in Western Oregon. Of special interest is this publication's focus on the history of the most important gold mines in the Little North Santiam Mining District. Illustrated with hard to find historical photos. 102 ppgs, 14.99

<u>The Economic Geological Resources of Oregon</u> - Unavailable since 1912, this publication offers rare insights into the early history of mining in Oregon. Included is hard to find information on gold, silver, copper and other mines that operated in Oregon at the turn of the century. 126 ppgs, 14.99

<u>Sights in the Gold Region of Oregon and California</u> - Unavailable since 1853, this publication provides a fascinating insight into the California and Oregon Gold Rushes through the eyes of one of the men who went West and "saw the elephant" to take part in it. Theodore Taylor Johnson's memoir of his journey to the gold fields of California and Oregon offers a unique look into this important time during the settling of the Far West. 382 ppgs, 24.99

South Dakota Mining Books

<u>Mining and Metallurgy of the Black Hills of South Dakota</u> - Mining historian Kerby Jackson introduces us to a classic mining work in this important re-issue of "Papers Read Before The Black Hills Mining Men's Association At Their Regularly Monthly Meeting On The Mining and Metallurgy of the Black Hills Ores". Unavailable since 1904, this publication offers rare insights into the famous bLack Hills mining region of South Dakota. Topics include Mining and Milling Methods of the Black Hills, South Dakota Gold Production, Some Features of the Mining Operations in the Homestake Mine at Lead, South Dakota, The Metallurgy of the Ore in the Homestake Mine, Cyanidation of Black Hills Ores, Wet Crushing of Ores in Solution, Cyaniding Practices at the Maitland Mine, Pyrite Ores and Their Smelting, Matte Smelting, Mining in the Bald Mountain and Ruby Districts of the Black Hills of South Dakota and more. Lavishly illustrated with rare historical photographs. **8.5" X 11", 162 ppgs, Retail Price: $14.99**

Utah Mining Books

Fluorite in Utah - Unavailable since 1954, this publication was originally compiled by the USGS, State of Utah and U.S. Atomic Energy Commission and details the mining of fluorspar, also known as fluorite in the State of Utah. Included are details on the geology and history of fluorspar (fluorite) mining in Utah, including details on where this unique gem mineral may be found in the State of Utah. **8.5" X 11", 60 ppgs. Retail Price: $8.99**

The Gold Hill Mining District of Utah - First published in 1935, it has been unavailable since those days and sheds important light on the mines, history and geology of Utah's Gold Hill Mining District. Included are rare insights into this important mining area, including the locations, histories and details of numerous mines. This volume is well illustrated with geological diagrams, as well as hard to find maps of some of the most important mines in this district. 202 ppgs., 19.99

The Mines, Miners and Minerals of Utah - First published in 1896, it has been unavailable since those days and sheds important light on the early mines and miners of Pioneer Utah, as well as the minerals which they won from the earth by laborious hard physical labor and sheer determination. Included are rare insights into the early mining history of Utah, as well details on hundreds of gold, silver and copper mines. 376 ppgs., 24.99

Washington Mining Books

The Republic Mining District of Washington - Unavailable since 1910, this important publication was originally published by the Washington Geologic Survey and has been unavailable for a century. Topics include the geology, rock formations and the formation of ore deposits in this important mining area of Washington State. Also included are hard to find details on the geology, history and locations of dozens of mines in the area. Some of the mines featured include the New Republic Mine, Ben Hur, Morning Glory, the South Republic Mine, Quilp, Surprise, Black Tail, Lone Pine, San Poil, Mountain Lion, Tom Thumb, Elcaliph and many others. **8.5" X 11", 94 ppgs, Retail Price: $10.99**

The Myers Creek and Nighthawk Mining Districts of Washington - Unavailable since 1911, this important publication was originally published by the Washington Geologic Survey and has been unavailable for a century. Topics include the geology, rock formations and the formation of ore deposits in these important mining areas of Washington State. Also included are hard to find details on the geology, history and locations of dozens of mines in the area. Some of the mines featured include the Grant Mine, Monterey, Nip and Tuck, Myers Creek, Number Nine, Neutral, Rainbow, Aztec, Crystal Butte, Apex, Butcher Boy, Molson, Mad River, Olentangy, Delate, Kelsey, Golden Chariot, Okanogan, Ohio, Forty-Ninth Parallel, Nighthawk, Favorite, Little Chopaka, Summit, Number One, California, Peerless, Caaba, Prize Group, Ruby, Mountain Sheep, Golden Zone, Rich Bar, Similkameen, Kimberly, Triune, Hiawatha, Trinity, Hornsilver, Maquae, Bellevue, Bullfrog, Palmer Lake, Ivanhoe, Copper World and many others.
  8.5" X 11", 136 ppgs, Retail Price: $12.99

The Blewett Mining District of Washington - Unavailable since 1911, this important publication was originally published by the Washington Geologic Survey and has been unavailable for a century. Topics include the geology, rock formations and the formation of ore deposits in this important mining area of Washington State. Also included are hard to find details on the geology, history and locations of dozens of mines in the area. Some of the mines featured include the Washington Meteor, Alta Vista, Pole Pick, Blinn, North Star, Golden Eagle, Tip Top, Wilder, Golden Guinea, Lucky Queen, Blue Bell, Prospect, Homestake, Lone Rock, Johnson, and others. **8.5" X 11", 134 ppgs, Retail Price: $12.99**

Silver Mining In Washington - Unavailable since 1955, this important publication was originally published by the Washington Geologic Survey. Featured are the hard to find locations and details pertaining to Washington's silver mines. **8.5" X 11", 180 ppgs, Retail Price: $15.99**

The Mines of Snohomish County Washington - Unavailable since 1942, this important publication was originally published by the Washington Geologic Survey and has been unavailable for seventy years. Featured are details on a large number of gold, silver, copper, lead and other metallic mineral mines. Included are the locations of each historic mine, along with information on the commodity produced. **8.5" X 11", 98 ppgs, Retail Price: $10.99**

The Mines of Chelan County Washington - Unavailable since 1943, this important publication was originally published by the Washington Geologic Survey and has been unavailable for seventy years. Featured are details on a large number of gold, silver, copper, lead and other metallic mineral mines. Included are the locations of each historic mine, along with information on the commodity. **8.5" X 11", 88 ppgs, Retail Price: $9.99**

Metal Mines of Washington - Unavailable since 1921, this important publication was originally published by the Washington Geologic Survey and has been unavailable for nearly ninety years. Widely considered a masterpiece on the Washington Mining Industry, "Metal Mines of Washington" sheds light on the important details of Washington's early mining years. Featured are details on hundreds of gold, silver, copper, lead and other metallic mineral mines. Included are hard to find details on the mineral resources of this state, as well as the locations of historic mines. Lavishly illustrated with maps and historic photos and complete with a glossary to explain any technical terms found in the text, this is one of the most important works on mining in the State of Washington. No prospector or miner should be without it if they are interested in mining in Washington. **8.5" X 11", 396 ppgs, Retail Price: $24.99**

Gem Stones In Washington - Unavailable since 1949, this important publication was originally published by the Washington Geologic Survey and has been unavailable since first published. Included are details on where to find naturally occurring gem stones in the State of Washington, including quartz crystal, amethyst, smoky quartz, milky quartz, agates, bloodstone, carnelian, chert, flint, jasper, onyx, petrified wood, opal, fire opal, hyalite and others. **8.5" X 11", 54 ppgs, Retail Price: $8.99**

The Covada Mining District of Washington - Unavailable since 1913, this important publication was originally published by the Washington Geologic Survey and has been unavailable for a century. Topics include the geology, rock formations and the formation of ore deposits in this important mining area of Washington State. Also included are hard to find details on the geology, history and locations of dozens of mines in the area. Some of the mines featured include the Admiral, Advance, Algonkian, Big Bug, Big Chief, Big Joker, Black Hawk, Black Tail, Black Thorn, Captain, Cherokee Strip, Colorado, Dan Patch, Dead Shot, Etta, Good Ore, Greasy Run, Great Scott, Idora, IXL, Jay Bird, Kentucky Bell, King Solomon, Laurel, Laura S, Little Jay, Meteor, Neglected, Northern Light, Old Nell, Plymouth Rock, Polaris, Quandary, Reserve, Shoo Fly, Silver Plume, Three Pines, Vernie, White Rose and dozens of others. **8.5" X 11", 114 ppgs, Retail Price: $10.99**

The Index Mining District of Washington - Unavailable since 1912, this important publication was originally published by the Washington Geologic Survey and has been unavailable for a century. Topics include the geology, rock formations and the formation of ore deposits in this important mining area of Washington State. Also included are hard to find details on the geology, history and locations of dozens of mines in the area. Some of the mines featured include the Sunset, Non-Pareil, Ethel Consolidated, Kittaning, Merchant, Homestead, Co-operative, Lost Creek, Uncle Sam, Calumet, Florence-Rae, Bitter Creek, Index Peacock, Gunn Peak, Helena, North Star, Buckeye. Copper Bell, Red Cross and others. **8.5" X 11", 114 ppgs, Retail Price: $11.99**

Mining & Mineral Resources of Stevens County Washington - Unavailable since 1920, this important publication was originally published by the Washington Geologic Survey and has been unavailable for a century. Topics include the geology, rock formations and the formation of ore deposits in these important mining areas of Washington State. Also included are hard to find details on the geology, history and locations of hundreds of mines in the area. **8.5" X 11", 372 ppgs, Retail Price: $24.99**

The Mines and Geology of the Loomis Quadrangle Okanogan County, Washington - Unavailable since 1972, this important publication was originally published by the Washington Geologic Survey and has been unavailable for a century. Topics include the geology, rock formations and the formation of ore deposits in this important mining area of Washington State. Also included are hard to find details on the geology, history and locations of dozens of gold, copper, silver and other mines in the area. **8.5" X 11", 150 ppgs, Retail Price: $12.99**

The Conconully Mining District of Okanogan County Washington - Unavailable since 1973, this important publication was originally published by the Washington Geologic Survey and has been unavailable for a century. Topics include the geology, rock formations and the formation of ore deposits in this important mining area of Washington State, which also includes Salmon Creek, Blue Lake and Galena. Also included are hard to find details on the geology, mining history and locations of dozens of mines in the area. Some of the mines include Arlington, Fourth of July, Sonny Boy, First Thought, Last Chance, War Eagle-Peacock, Wheeler, Mohawk, Lone Star, Woo Loo Moo Loo, Keystone, Hughes, Plant-Callahan, Johnny Boy, Leuena, Gubser, John Arthur, Tough Nut, Homestake, Key and many others **8.5" X 11", 68 ppgs, Retail Price: $8.99**

Gold Hunting in the Cascade Mountains of Washington - First published in 1861, this rare publication offers rare insights into an early search for placer gold near Mount Saint Helens in what was then Washington Territory. This rare booklet was written by an anonymous author under the name Loo-Wit Lat-Kla, which is a Native American word for "fire mountain," referring to Mount St. Helens. Gold Hunting in the Cascade Mountains is a fascinating read on the early history of mining in Washington, as well as on the mountaineering of Mount St. Helens. Only one copy of the original text survives. In the 1950's a limited edition of 300 copies was produced by Yale University, few of which still survive today.**8.5" X 11", 56 ppgs, Retail Price: $8.99**

Wyoming Mining Books

Mining in the Laramie Basin of Wyoming - Unavailable since 1909, this publication was originally compiled by the United States Department of Interior. Also included are insights into the mineralization and other characteristics of this important mining region, especially in regards to coal, limestone, gypsum, bentonite clay, cement, sand, clay and copper. **8.5" X 11", 104 ppgs, Retail Price: $11.99**

More Mining Books

Prospecting and Developing A Small Mine - Topics covered include the classification of varying ores, how to take a proper ore sample, the proper reduction of ore samples, alluvial sampling, how to understand geology as it is applied to prospecting and mining, prospecting procedures, methods of ore treatment, the application of drilling and blasting in a small mine and other topics that the small scale miner will find of benefit. **8.5" X 11", 112 ppgs, Retail Price: $11.99**

Timbering For Small Underground Mines - Topics covered include the selection of caps and posts, the treatment of mine timbers, how to install mine timbers, repairing damaged timbers, use of drift supports, headboards, squeeze sets, ore chute construction, mine cribbing, square set timbering methods, the use of steel and concrete sets and other topics that the small underground miner will find of benefit. This volume also includes twenty eight illustrations depicting the proper construction of mine timbering and support systems that greatly enhance the practical usability of the information contained in this small book. **8.5" X 11", 88 ppgs. Retail Price: $10.99**

Timbering and Mining - A classic mining publication on Hard Rock Mining by W.H. Storms. Unavailable since 1909, this rare publication provides an in depth look at American methods of underground mine timbering and mining methods. Topics include the selection and preservation of mine timbers, drifting and drift sets, driving in running ground, structural steel in mine workings, timbering drifts in gravel mines, timbering methods for driving shafts, positioning drill holes in shafts, timbering stations at shafts, drainage, mining large ore bodies by means of open cuts or by the "Glory Hole" system, stoping out ore in flat or low lying veins, use of the "Caving System", stoping in swelling ground, how to stope out large ore bodies, Square Set timbering on the Comstock and its modifications by California miners, the construction of ore chutes, stoping ore bodies by use of the "Block System", how to work dangerous ground, information on the "Delprat System" of stoping without mine timbers, construction and use of headframes and much more. This volume provides a reference into not only practical methods of mining and timbering that may be employed in narrow vein mining by small miners today, but also rare insights into how mines were being worked at the turn of the 19th Century. **8.5" X 11", 288 ppgs. Retail Price: $24.99**

A Study of Ore Deposits For The Practical Miner - Mining historian Kerby Jackson introduces us to a classic mining publication on ore deposits by J.P. Wallace. First published in 1908, it has been unavailable for over a century. Included are important insights into the properties of minerals and their identification, on the occurrence and origin of gold, on gold alloys, insights into gold bearing sulfides such as pyrites and arsenopyrites, on gold bearing vanadium, gold and silver tellurides, lead and mercury tellurides, on silver ores, platinum and iridium, mercury ores, copper ores, lead ores, zinc ores, iron ores, chromium ores, manganese ores, nickel ores, tin ores, tungsten ores and others. Also included are facts regarding rock forming minerals, their composition and occurrences, on igneous, sedimentary, metamorphic and intrusive rocks, as well as how they are geologically disturbed by dikes, flows and faults, as well as the effects of these geologic actions and why they are important to the miner. Written specifically with the common miner and prospector in mind, the book will help to unlock the earth's hidden wealth for you and is written in a simple and concise language that anyone can understand. **8.5" X 11", 366 ppgs. Retail Price: $24.99**

Mine Drainage - Unavailable since 1896, this rare publication provides an in depth look at American methods of underground mine drainage and mining pump systems. This volume provides a reference into not only practical methods of mining drainage that may be employed in narrow vein mining by small miners today, but also rare insights into how mines were being worked at the turn of the 19th Century. **8.5" X 11", 218 ppgs. Retail Price: $24.99**

Fire Assaying Gold, Silver and Lead Ores - Unavailable since 1907, this important publication was originally published by the Mining and Scientific Press and was designed to introduce miners and prospectors of gold, silver and lead to the art of fire assaying. Topics include the fire assaying of ores and products containing gold, silver and lead; the sampling and preparation of ore for an assay; care of the assay office, assay furnaces; crucibles and scorifiers; assay balances; metallic ores; scorification assays; cupelling; parting' crucible assays, the roasting of ores and more. This classic provides a time honored method of assaying put forward in a clear, concise and easy to understand language that will make it a benefit to even beginners. **8.5" X 11", 96 ppgs. Retail Price: $11.99**

Methods of Mine Timbering - Originally published in 1896, this important publication on mining engineering has not been available for nearly a century. Included are rare insights into historical methods of timbering structural support that were used in underground metal mines during the California that still have a practical application for the small scale hardrock miner of today. **8.5" X 11", 94 ppgs. Retail Price: $10.99**

The Enrichment of Copper Sulfide Ores - First published in 1913, it has been unavailable for over a century. Topics include the definition and types of ore enrichment, the oxidation of copper ores, the precipitation of metallic sulfides. Also included are the results of dozens of lab experiments pertaining to the enrichment of sulfide ores that will be of interest to the practical hard rock mine operator in his efforts to release the metallic bounty from his mine's ore. **8.5" X 11", 92 ppgs. Retail Price: $9.99**

A Study of Magmatic Sulfide Ores - Unavailable since 1914, this rare publication provides an in depth look at magmatic sulfide ores. Some of the topics included are the definition and classification of magmatic ores, descriptions of some magmatic sulfide ore deposits known at the time of publication including copper and nickel bearing pyrrohitic ore bodies, chalcopyrite-bornite deposits, pyritic deposits, magnetite-ileminite deposits, chromite deposits and magmatic iron ore deposits. Also included are details on how to recognize these types of ore deposits while prospecting for valuable hardrock minerals. **8.5" X 11", 138 ppgs. Retail Price: $11.99**

The Cyanide Process of Gold Recovery - Unavailable since 1894 and released under the name "The Cyanide Process: Its Practical Application and Economical Results", this rare publication provides an in depth look at the early use of cyanide leaching for gold recovery from hardrock mine ores. This volume provides a reference into the early development and use of cyanide leaching to recover gold. **8.5" X 11", 162 ppgs. Retail Price: $14.99**

California Gold Milling Practices - Unavailable since 1895 and released under the name "California Gold Practices", this rare publication provides an in depth look at early methods of milling used to reduce gold ores in California during the late 19th century. This volume provides a reference into the early development and use of milling equipment during the earliest years of the California Gold Rush up to the age of the Industrial Revolution. Much of the information still applies today and will be of use to small scale miners engaging in hardrock mining. **8.5" X 11", 104 ppgs. Retail Price: $10.99**

Leaching Gold and Silver Ores With The Plattner and Kiss Processes - Mining historian Kerby Jackson introduces us to a classic mining publication on the evaluation and examination of mines and prospects by C.H. Aaron. First published in 1881, it has been unavailable for over a century and sheds important light on the leaching of gold and silver ores with the Plattner and Kiss processes. **8.5" X 11", 204 ppgs. Retail Price: $15.99**

The Metallurgy of Lead and the Desilverization of Base Bullion - First published in 1896, it has been unavailable for over a century and sheds important light on the the recovery of silver from lead based ores. Some of the topics include the properties of lead and some of its compounds, lead ores such as galenite, anglesite, cerussite and others, the distribution of lead ores throughout the United States and the sampling and assaying of lead ores. Also covered is the metallurgical treatment of lead ores, as well as the desilverization of lead by the Pattinson Process and the Parkes Process. Hofman's text has long been considered one of the most important early works on the recovery of silver from lead based ores. 8.5" X 11", 452 ppgs. Retail Price: $29.99

Ore Sampling For Small Scale Miners - First published in 1916, it has been unavailable for over a century and sheds important light on historic methods of ore sampling in hardrock mines. Topics include how to take correct ore samples and the conditions that affect sampling, such as their subdivision and uniformity. Particular detail is given to methods of hand sampling ore bodies by grab sample, pipe sample and coning, as well as sampling by mechanical methods. Also given are insights into the screening, drying and grinding processes to achieve the most consistent sample results and much more. 8.5" X 11", 124 ppgs. Retail Price: $12.99

The Extraction of Silver, Copper and Tin from Ores - First published in 1896, it has been unavailable for over a century and sheds important light on how historic miners recovered silver, copper and tin from their mining operations. The book is split into three sections, including a discussion on the Lixiviation of Silver Ores, the mining and treatment of copper ores as practiced at Tharsis, Spain and the smelting of tin as it was practiced by metallurgists at Pulo Brani, Singapore. Also included is an overview and analysis of these historic metal recovery methods that will be of benefit to those interested in the extraction of silver, copper and tin from small mines. 8.5" X 11", 118 ppgs. Retail Price: $14.99

The Roasting of Gold and Silver Ores - First published in 1880, it has been unavailable for over a century and sheds important light on how historic miners recovered gold and silver rom their mining operations. Topics include details on the most important silver and free milling gold ores, methods of desulphurization of ores, methods of deoxidation, the chlorination of ores, methods and details on roasting gold and silver ores, notes on furnaces and more. Also included are details on numerous methods of gold and silver recovery, including the Ottokar Hofman's Process, the Patera Process, Kiss Process, Augustin Process, Ziervogel Process and others. 8.5" X 11", 178 ppgs. Retail Price: $19.99

The Examination of Mines and Prospects - First published in 1912, it has been unavailable for over a century and sheds important light on how to examine and evaluate hardrock mines, prospects and lode mining claims. Sections include Mining Examinations, Structural Geology, Structural Features of Ore Deposits, Primary Ores and their Distribution, Types of Primary Ore Deposits, Primary Ore Shoots, The Primary Alteration of Wall Rocks, Alterations by Surface Agencies, Residual Ores and their Distribution, Secondary Ores and Ore Shoots and Vein Outcrops. This hard to find information is a must for those who are interested in owning a mine or who already own a lode mining claim and wish to succeed at quartz mining. 8.5" X 11", 250 ppgs. Retail Price: $19.99

Garnets: Their Mining, Milling and Utilization - First published in 1925, it has been unavailable since those days and sheds important light on the mining, milling and utilization of garnets. Included are details on the characteristics of garnets, where they are found and how they were mined. 78 ppgs, 10.99

Gemstones and Precious Stones of North America - Leading mining historian Kerby Jackson introduces us to a classic mining publication on the gems and precious stones of the United States, Canada and mexico. First published in 1890, it has been unavailable since those days and sheds important light on the gems and precious stones that may be found in North America. Included are chapters on diamonds, corundum, sapphire, ruby, topaz, emerald, disapore, spinel, turquoise, tourmaline, garnets, beyrl, peridot, zircon, quartz crystals, feldspars, pearls and many others. Included are details on where these gems and precious stones may be found throughout North America, as well as their characteristics. 360 ppgs, 24.99

Mining Camps and Mining Districts - First released in 1885 by Charles Howard Shinn under the title "Mining Camps: A Study in American Frontier Government", this publication offers a unique look at how early gold miners established their own forms of representative government during the California Gold Rush. Drawing on the the early mining codes of mideviel German miners in the Harz Mountains, on the mining customs of the Cornish tin miners and early Spanish mining laws introduced into California, the miners established the first governments in the American West. 340 ppgs, 24.99

BLM Field Handbook for Mineral Examiners - Leading mining historian Kerby Jackson introduces us to a classic mining publication on mine evaluation. First published in 1962, this work sheds important light on the techniques of BLM Mineral Examiners to perform validity on mining claims. 132 ppgs, 10.99

<u>Six Months In The Gold Mines During The California Gold Rush</u> - Unavailable since 1850, this important work is a first hand account of one "49'ers" personal experience during the great California Gold Rush, shedding important light on one of the most exciting periods in the history of not only California, but also the world. Compiled from journals written between 1847 and 1849 by E. Gould Buffum, a native of New York, "Six Months In The Gold Mines During The California Gold Rush" offers a rare look into the day to day lives of the people who came to California to work in her gold mines when the state was still a great frontier. 8.5" X 11", 290 ppgs. Retail Price: $19.99

<u>The Discovery of Gold in Australia</u> - First published in 1852, it has been unavailable since those days and sheds important light on Australia's gold mining history. Included are rare communications between British agents and the British Crown when gold was first discovered in Australia in 1851. This rare text contains hard to find details on Australia's first mining camps and Britain's early attempts to provide for the orderly regulation of gold mines in that part of the world. Also of interest are hard to find extracts of articles that appeared in the early colonial newspapers that did their best to report on Australia's gold rush as it took place.
102 ppgs, 10.99

<u>Notes on Ore Sampling in Mines</u> - Unavailable since 1903, this publication offers rare insights into how ore was sampled in metallic mineral mines at the turn of the 19th Century. Included in this small booklet are facts about how to take, separate and handle an ore sample, as well as details on some of the equipment that was used for sampling in the old days.
68 ppgs, 7.99

<u>Elementary Methods of Placer Gold Mining</u> - Unavailable since 1944, this publication offers rare insights into the art of finding and recovering placer gold. Included in this small booklet are facts about the geology of alluvial gold deposits, the various types of placer gold deposits and the metals associated with placer gold. Also included are basic instructions on panning for gold, the use of sluice boxes, rocker boxes, as well as the recovery of fine gold by amalgamation plates and other methods. Basic plans to build your own mining equipment is also included. Written mainly for miners in Idaho, this short booklet also includes an overview of where to find gold in Idaho.
58 ppgs, 7.99

<u>Mining Districts of the Western United States</u> - Unavailable since 1912, this publication provides the locations and other basic information on the mining districts of the Western United States. This important reference book provides valuable insights into the general locations of where gold, silver, copper and other mines have operated in the Western States. This fascinating book offers a rare glimpse into these marvels of early mining technology that once helped early miners win millions of ounces of gold and silver from the hills of the Far West. 336 ppgs, 24.99

<u>Some Facts About Ore Deposits</u> - Written in 1935, this hard to find publication includes valuable facts on the nature of metallic ore deposits. Highlighted here are the details on how ores are deposited, on the fallacy that ore deposits always increase in value with depth, primary ore zones, myths regarding the leaching of ores, facts about secondary ore enrichment, which rocks are associated with which types of metals and much more. This small booklet will be found to be of immense value to the miner who is looking to learn about hard rock mining. 126 ppgs, 11.99

<u>Prospecting Field Tests For The Common Metals</u> - Written in 1942, this hard to find publication includes valuable facts on how to identify common metals in the field. Included are field tests for gold, silver, copper, arsenic, antimony, iron, chromium, manganese, lead, cobalt, nickel, tin, tungsten, zinc, vanadium and many other minerals utilizing reagents, blowpipes and other methods. This small booklet will be found to be of immense value to the miner who is looking to learn about hard rock mining. 82 ppgs, 8.99

<u>Sampling for Gold</u> - Leading mining historian Kerby Jackson brings together five historic publications from the Arizona Bureau of Mines on the subject of sampling and testing for gold, be it placer or lode gold. Included in this publication are "Mill and Smelter Methods of Sampling" (1915), "Sampling and the Estimation of Gold in a Placer Deposit" (1917), "Sampling of Ore Dumps and Tailings" (1917), "Sampling Mineralized Veins" (1918) and "Select Blowpipe and Acid Tests for Minerals" (1918). As sampling is the most important activity that a miner or prospector seeking gold needs to engage in, these tried and proven methods of sampling will be found to greatly assist those seeking their own golden fortune. 86 ppgs, 10.99

<u>Treating Gold Ores</u> - Written in 1932, this hard to find publication includes valuable facts about the handling of ores from gold mines. Included in this short publication is an overview of smelting, milling, amalgamation, gravity stamp milling, the use of retorts, the refining of bullion from retorts, use of ball mills, huntington mills and arrastras, as well as details on cyanidation, gravity concentration and flotation. This publication is a must for anyone looking to develop a small gold mine. 90 ppgs, 9.99

<u>Selling Mines and Prospects</u> - Leading mining historian Kerby Jackson introduces us to a classic mining publication on the selling of mines and prospects. Written in 1918, this hard to find publication includes valuable facts about how mines and prospects were sold in decades past that will still be found to be of use today. 46 ppgs, 7.99

<u>Mining Stamp Mills</u> - Unavailable since 1912, this publication offers rare insights into the development and use of stamp mills that were once employed in gold and other mines in the century past. Included are details on the history of stamp mills, including their evolution from the Cornish Mill, Appalachian Mill and the California Mill, as well as the construction and operation of these mills in mining operations. This fascinating book offers a rare glimpse into these marvels of early mining technology that once helped early miners win millions of ounces of gold and silver from the hills of the Far West. 164 ppgs, 14.99

<u>Notes on Ore Sampling in Mines</u> - Unavailable since 1903, this publication offers rare insights into how ore was sampled in metallic mineral mines at the turn of the 19th Century. Included in this small booklet are facts about how to take, separate and handle an ore sample, as well as details on some of the equipment that was used for sampling in the old days. 68 ppgs, 7.99

Made in the USA
Middletown, DE
01 February 2023

23370728R00049